D1570422

THE WORST TIMES ARE THE BEST TIMES

The Championship Coach Shares Inspiring Stories of Overcoming Adversity to Eventually Lead N.C. Central University to its First Division I NCAA Tournament

LEVELLE MOTON

AND EDWARD G. ROBINSON III

MR PUBLISHING

MR Publishing, LLC
Washington, D.C.

First published by MR Publishing, LLC

©2014 LeVelle Moton and Edward G. Robinson III

MR Publishing, LLC
Address: 3401 12th Street, NE #4413
Washington, D.C. 20017
Phone: 919-200-5510
Email: info@mrpublishingllc.com
Web: mrpublishingllc.com
ISBN: 978-0-692-21178-6

Trade distribution:
In the U.S. through Small Press United

Special discounts are available for bulk purchases by organizations and
institutions. Please contact MR Publishing, LLC for more information by
phone or email.

Special discounts are also available for speaking engagement bookings
for LeVelle Moton or Edward G. Robinson III. Please contact Angelique
D. Stallings at angelique@mochamindagency.com or 919-539-3320.

Editor: Adrienne Johnson Martin
Copy editor: Sheon Ladson Wilson
Layout design: Victoria Valentine

Cover photo courtesy of North Carolina Central University

Printed in the United States.

To my Lord and Savior Jesus Christ: I'm nothing without you. Thank you for never giving up on me. Philippians 4:13

To my wife Bridget: From five people sitting in the gym to sold out arenas, you've been with me every step of the way. I Love you!

To my mother Hattie McDougald: Your Love, support and strength made me who I am. My only goal in life was to make you proud.

To my brother Verne: Your tough Love made me a winner!

To my grandmother Mattie McDougald: Continue to be my angel. God rest your precious soul.

To my children Brooke & Velle Jr.: Everything I do, I do it for you. Daddy Loves you!

– L.M.

To my wife, Candice Watkins Robinson, who insisted that I write this book and supported me when I did: my love is eternal.
— E.G.R. III

Sometimes we must be hurt in order to grow.
Sometimes we must fail in order to know.
Sometimes we must lose in order to gain
Because some lessons in life are best learned through pain.
– Unknown Poet

CONTENTS

x   About LeVelle Moton

xii   Forewords:

   xii   Duke's Mike Krzyzewski

   xiii N.C. State's Mark Gottfried

   xiv   North Carolina's Roy Williams

1   Introduction

9   Prologue

19   Chapter 1   Fatherless

37   Chapter 2   New Edition

53   Chapter 3   Strike Three

65   Chapter 4   Guardian Angel

81   Chapter 5   Hot Shot

97   From Coach Moton's Photo Album

111 Chapter 6   Choices, Decisions and Consequences

127 Chapter 7   Lunch Ticket (A Love Story)

143 Chapter 8   First Time

153 Chapter 9   Playground Legend

175 Chapter 10   Somebody Prayed For Me

215 Chapter 11   Going To Meet Jay-Z
                      (As Told By 9th Wonder)

231 Afterword: Mike Tomlin

233 Q&A: New Edition

225 Acknowledgements

227 About the Author

229 Resource Guide

LEVELLE MOTON

LeVelle De'Shea Moton has pursued success since the day he was born. The Boston native, who was raised in Raleigh, N.C. by a single mother, underwent tough times in one of the city's most notorious housing projects. Despite the environment of a crime- and drug-infested neighborhood, he learned the importance of hard work and persistence. With his grandmother's love and his mother's discipline, he blossomed into one of the country's most successful up-and-coming NCAA Division I college basketball coaches, as well as a loving husband, doting father and God-fearing man.

Moton is a graduate of North Carolina Central University, where he was a standout basketball player for the Eagles. He graduated in 1996 after becoming the third all-time leading scorer in school history – 1,714 points. Named to the university's Hall of Fame in 2004, he returned to his alma mater in 2007 as an assistant coach. In 2009, he was hired as the 17th head coach.

In his fifth season as head coach, Moton led the school to its first Mid-Eastern Athletic Conference Tournament Championship and a berth into its first men's Division I NCAA Tournament. To culminate that tremendous 2013-14 season, he was named MEAC Coach of the Year.

Moton, who played four years overseas as a professional, is known for his prolific shooting as a guard for N.C. Central. He averaged 21.3

points per game as a senior and was named CIAA Player of the Year, capturing the award over Virginia Union University standout and future NBA player Ben Wallace; he was the first player in school history to earn that honor. He earned the nickname "Poetry 'n Moton," finishing his collegiate career with an 80-28 record.

His achievements led him to a brief stint in 1996 with the Seattle Supersonics of the NBA. Later, he played professionally in Indonesia, Germany, Cyprus and Israel.

After his playing days were over, Moton turned his attention to teaching and coaching. He started his coaching career at West Millbrook Middle School in Raleigh in 2001, moved to Sanderson High School in 2004 and eventually into the college ranks in 2007. He is a graduate of Enloe High School in Raleigh, where he spent the majority of his childhood. At Enloe High School, he became a McDonald's All-American nominee while winning three conference tournaments, Wake County Player of the Year, All-State selection, and averaging 30 points per game with a school record 51 points and CAP 5 Conference Player of the Year.

Moton champions himself as more than a basketball coach, holding higher education as a priority for players and for himself. He earned a master's degree from N.C. Central in special education in December 2013. He also has led a charitable life, forming the non-profit Velle Cares Foundation, Inc., and hosting an annual community day at the Raleigh Boys & Girls Club. The Velle Cares Foundation's mission is to serve and assist community-based organizations that promote health, education and life skills for children and families in at-risk situations.

Moton and his wife Bridget live in Durham, N.C., with their daughter Brooke and son LeVelle Jr.

FOREWORD

by
Coach Mike Krzyzewski
Duke University

 Whenever you are with LeVelle Moton you feel better. It has been a privilege for me to be LeVelle's friend for many years. I have had the opportunity to watch him grow from being a terrific player in college to an outstanding coach at the Division I level. During the time I have known him, I have asked myself the question, "How did he become so successful?" The answer to that question is really why this book is so important.

As a youngster, LeVelle was raised by a single-mom who gave him unfailing support and unconditional love. He used this as the foundation not only to have dreams, but to actually pursue those dreams. I believe this was the time in his life when he developed the self-motivation necessary to do the work that is required to turn dreams into reality. He did not allow obstacles to get in the way. He worked hard to overcome all the challenges that his life threw at him and he succeeded!

To read about the journey that LeVelle has taken is incredibly interesting. He is a "no-excuse" person. He never limited himself because of the neighborhood he was from and he never allowed the hardships of a difficult economic background to defeat him. His positive attitude and tremendous work ethic have combined to make him a successful coach and, more important, a truly good person. He is an excellent role model for youth and, especially, for young men. The advice that he gives in this book can be a huge help to so many on their journeys to success.

Being LeVelle's friend has made me a better person. I wish the same for the readers of his book.

FOREWORD

by

Coach Mark Gottfried

North Carolina State University

Regardless of where a coach starts, the road up the college basketball coaching ranks can be a challenging one. Our profession is a competitive one, and a lot of quality coaches across the country have fallen short of their dreams. When you factor in a young man traveling that road after growing up in housing projects, it's clear LeVelle Moton's story in "The Worst Times Are The Best Times" is an inspiring one. It's a classic example of what is possible when a man is committed to his vision.

The adversity of growing up in housing projects made LeVelle the coach he is today. But what's great about his story is that he has put the same effort giving back to others that he has put in becoming a winning basketball coach. On and off the court, he has committed to improving the lives of others.

I think what LeVelle is doing in the community is something everyone can learn from. He has shown that if you remain focused, you can overcome adversity and achieve your goals. That has become evident in how he leads his team and how he has developed into a rising presence in the college basketball coaching community.

FOREWORD

by
Coach Roy Williams
The University of North Carolina at Chapel Hill

 I encourage everyone to read this book about LeVelle Moton and listen to what he has to say. I know the experiences he's had during his life will provide great opportunities for someone to learn something you can apply to your own.

LeVelle's story is great to hear and can help anyone who has the desire to push, have self-discipline and be someone in a position of leadership for young people. I am an old guy, but I can learn a lot from LeVelle's story. I hope you will join me in learning something from him as well.

THE WORST TIMES ARE THE BEST TIMES

INTRODUCTION

*"Long live the rose that grew from con-
crete when no one else ever cared."*
Rapper Tupac Amaru Shakur

Before pre-season workouts begin at N.C. Central University, shortly after everyone arrives on campus following summer break, our team meets to discuss the upcoming season. After this initial team meeting, where rules are explained and the business of the season reviewed, I ask: How many of you are going to turn professional when you're done playing here?

Everyone in the room raises his hand. Talk inevitably turns to dreams of making the NBA.

I encourage all young people to dream big. But dream intelligently. Take all the facts into consideration and go after dreams with a realistic desire. Know which mountain you must climb to reach your goal. Be prepared.

So we play musical chairs. I set out 14 chairs for 15 players. We turn the music up in the gymnasium. Players start moving with the tentativeness of children, slowly circling the chairs, remembering the game from their youth. The music stops. One chair is taken away. Then another. I encourage them to play this game like it's the NCAA Tournament Finals. Barking instructions, I give incentives while creating commotion. Music blares. They start to laugh and have fun. Another chair disappears. Then another. Suddenly, the game becomes more serious. There are two chairs for three people.

In the end, there is just one winner. And that's the lesson. To make the NBA, one of my players has to win an equivalent game of musical chairs against 1.2 million other players, considering his competition from NCAA Division I, II and III schools, junior colleges and overseas professionals. Everyone is fighting for 30 NBA draft positions. Many second-round selections are cut. These are the facts.

Imagine that. Some of my players can't win a game of musical chairs in their own gym, with their favorite music playing, in a whimsical environment filled with laughter and cheer. Try winning musical chairs in a hostile environment with everything against you. Better yet, try beating out two veterans for one spot on an NBA roster.

I like to tell that story because it reminds me of my purpose as a coach and a teacher. I must tell the truth. We can't all play in the NBA. That's a simple fact. It's not meant to hurt anyone's feelings or dash their dreams. It's a statement I make so we can all communicate from the same planet. I'm here on Earth, where the competition for the best – of anything but the NBA in particular – is tough. Beyond tough. It's one of the most competitive career fields in the world.

I don't want to waste anyone's time talking about how to make it to the NBA. I'd rather share stories from my past that possibly relate to your future. If you're blessed to make the NBA or WNBA, you were given an exceptional talent. Still, you're human and must deal with day-to-day issues like the rest of us. It's these life lessons that dominate my book. I talk about mistakes made, friends lost, hungry nights, angry mornings, bullets dodged, thoughts confused, frustrations fought, wrong choices, right choices, fun times, late-night calls, mid-afternoon breakups, books read and points scored. All of these things are found in the chapters of my first book, "The Worst Times Are the Best Times."

Why Am I Writing This Book?

I pondered this question for several years before committing to put my thoughts on paper. I worried that I wasn't popular enough to write a book. I doubted I had something important enough to say. I've changed my mind, disregarding those fears, and I've developed a clear mind about my purpose. I've acknowledged that I have a unique voice and specific message to share.

So the stories you read are genuine. They come from the heart. They come from a place of understanding. In some ways, I might be like you: I come from the bottom and have certainly worked to a place of comfort, though I'm still reaching for the top. In contemplating these stories, I discovered a lot about myself, mostly that I was placed here on Earth to help change hearts and minds.

I've searched for moments that have shaped my life for the better and presented them here for you to share. This is not an autobiography. It's part-memoir. I'm sharing these stories because they were significant moments in my life that have some value for others. How much value depends on where you are in your life.

What Can You Expect?

God has been my source, my inspiration, and He's allowed me to overcome the highest form of dysfunction a human being could witness yet share those experiences with the world. And I'm grateful.

Everything I do is meant to help someone else. This is no different. This book offers inspiration and motivation, tools that helped me survive the projects as a child, college as a young man and the work world as a grown man.

Adult readers may relate to these stories from my childhood, because I'm not the only one who grew up without a father or lived in the projects or searched for respect or suffered with a broken heart. I find that stories have different morals for us as we grow and develop. Something your mother said to you when you were a child can resonate in a new way as an adult. I have written this to serve both audiences.

Young readers may find that they, too, relate to these stories and can find something special to grab ahold of as they read. They may identify with my experiences and use something from them to better their lives.

Perhaps the young and the old can talk about what they think and learn from each other. This type of communication is necessary if we are to understand one another. I tell stories about my childhood to my 5-year-old daughter Brooke all the time. Though she may not understand them fully, we manage to create some type of understanding, especially when it applies to candy. There are also times when she provides wisdom I never expected to hear from her mouth. Talking and listening are key.

I didn't write this book to showcase my knowledge of basketball or tactics. Basketball is what I do and not who I am. I want to share stories about life as it relates to sports. So in this book, I have written about what it's like to grow up as a black boy without a father and still become a successful man. I've described what it's like to follow the road less traveled. I've documented what it's like to fight for respect and demand it, but without dying for it. I've detailed what it's like to fail and then succeed. I have written what it's like to continue to have faith and overcome adversity when the world seems to close in on you. Each story offers a tale from my life that ends with a lesson learned in the "Inside the Locker Room" section and lessons to take away in the "Chalkboard" section. Some were difficult lessons, yet they built the foundation for my maturation. Others were easier to digest. Some of these stories were unresolved until I wrote this book. I learned something new by revisiting them.

I did not remember every detail, so I had some help reporting the facts. Though I tried to recall specifics from my past, some moments and environments needed to be revisited. Readers should expect a break from my voice as details are revealed in the form of journalism. My friend, journalist Edward G. Robinson III, supported my memory with reporting and fact-checking.

My years as a high school teacher taught me that everyone has different learning styles. My style is visual and so that's how I present material. I'm a child of the 1980s and 90s, and poetry and hip-hop are always at my disposal. My love of the arts, particularly hip-hop music, helps me relate to today's player. Mostly I'm a straight-talker, an educated teacher who will use the best resources to communicate my message.

I coach college basketball in one of the most competitive states in America. I grew up watching N.C. State, UNC, Duke and Wake Forest form heated rivalries in the ACC that continue to this day. I coach in the heart of Tobacco Road, among Mark Gottfried at N.C. State, Roy Williams at UNC and Mike Krzyzewski at Duke. I am, however, different from those coaches because I don't land the one-and-done, off-to-the-NBA, blue-collar recruits who will make millions and retire at 37. My players must concentrate on being student-athletes from the day they arrive on campus. I am very clear with them about why they have enrolled and what I expect. I focus on the development of the man. I know that as soon as they leave campus, they must compete in society. They probably won't have a long-term professional basketball contract to take care of their families or the contacts to start a prosperous broadcasting career.

I have to instill the proper values in these young men because they are going to be heads of households, fathers and future leaders. I have to make sure that when the ball stops bouncing they are prepared to be productive citizens.

I remember watching television as a kid – four or five – and thinking, "God gave them something special." I thought he gave the actors on television something he didn't give me. He must have. Their worlds were so different from mine. I looked out the window at the Boston skyline and everything seemed so far way from the projects in Orchard Park. The lights were close, yet they were twinkling far away. I really didn't think I had a chance in life.

But I soon learned that this world offers you an opportunity to be successful. That word "successful" is tricky because people define success in many ways. Most define it in a materialistic or superficial way, meaning the type of Jordans you wear or the type of car you drive or the size of your home. I learned that wasn't the only type of success. Success is taking the cards you were dealt and making the best hand possible. Born in the projects? So what? Become a lawyer. Born without a father in the home? So what? Become a college professor. Born with less? So what? Become a real-estate magnate.

The world is filled with people hanging on corners or locked in prison who didn't believe. They gave up. That dude standing on the corner, he didn't raise his hand in eighth grade and say, "I want to be homeless." Something happened along the way. I'm willing to bet, despite what life handed him or whatever curveball was thrown, he gave up. He saw a glimpse of a brighter future and convinced himself it was too hard to obtain. Convince yourself otherwise.

You have an opportunity to be successful in this world. At the end of the day, that opportunity falls back on you. How will you act? How hard will you work? Will you rise above obstacles? Will you see the angles? Will you persevere? Will you become that "rose that grew from concrete when no one else ever cared?"

That's a line from my favorite poem, written by the late Tupac Shakur. Its message is simple yet so meaningful, especially in the way that it encapsulates my life. I am that rose that grew from concrete. I am that soul that sprouted unexpectedly from rugged, harsh surroundings, my petals worn but still soft and beautiful. If you think in terms of statistics and news reports, I was not supposed to make it in society, but I did. I thrived. With love and support – water that helped me grow – I inched through the cracks and now stand tall like that rose. I know that there are others born beneath the same concrete, who with similar heart and determination have defied the odds and grown petals too. I have a few words to encourage them.

PROLOGUE

"Waking up in a dream
Sleepwalking on another big stage
You never heard peace 'til you hear people scream
Your name in unison, I'm so far away
From the place I used to be, struggling usually
Look at the newer me, fate pursuing me
I can feel the energy in the air
It feel like I'm supposed to be here."
Rapper Kendrick Lamar, "Now or Never,"
from "good kid, m.A.A.d city"

I was sitting in my office at N.C. Central University on March 18, 2014, preparing for my appearance in two days on what was going to be the biggest stage of my basketball life when I received a phone call from my wife Bridget. She told me that my 1-year-old son, LeVelle Jr., had spilled hot coffee on himself. My mother, his caretaker, had tried to reach me by cell phone, but I had left it in the car. Mom explained to Bridget that V.J. had blisters on his face.

"What?" I said to my wife.

"He's okay," she said.

Emergency Room

I was consumed with work, busy as a Los Angeles freeway. I was reviewing film, conducting media interviews, filing paperwork and darting in and out of meetings, all while preparing a game plan for our trip to San Antonio. The men's basketball team had earned a berth into the Division I NCAA Tournament for the first time in school history. We were scheduled to face Iowa State on that Thursday in the second round in the AT&T Center, and we had chartered a plane to leave Wednesday afternoon.

The campus buzzed with excitement; positive energy radiated all around me. My phone rang incessantly while people knocked at the door every 10 minutes. Still, something felt amiss, uncomfortable. I sat there thinking. My mother, bless her heart, is from the old school, which means she's not taking you to the emergency room unless you're dead. I knew what to do: I switched into my father role. I arrived home in record time, where I found my mother holding my son in her arms, his face irritated from the hot coffee.

His face grew progressively worse. I rushed him to the urgent care facility near our home. My wife remained at work because she thought the situation was stable. As I buckled my son into his car seat, I photographed his face and shot her a text, apprising her of the severity of the situation. The photo, which disturbs me to think about, showed the skin on his face puckering, his eyes swollen and his face discolored and bloated. It appeared to be more than just blisters, and it seemed serious.

My worries were confirmed by the frightened looks of the nurses at the urgent care center. They held their faces in disbelief and immediately called an ambulance to take V.J. to the emergency burn unit at UNC Hospital. That reaction scared me, but I was trying to be strong for my son and my wife. She arrived panicked, which escalated to hysterical, and eventually she fell out, unable to look at my son's weary little face. They took her out of the room. V.J. opened his eyes, saw his mother leaving and went berserk, calling for her.

It was a crazy scene, our son crying amid nurses, doctors and strangers alerted by the noise. By mid-afternoon, we were distressed and exhausted. Fearing the worse, unclear about our son's condition, we prayed for mercy. My wife rode to the hospital with V.J., while I drove. As they wheeled him on a stretcher to a room, his face tightened, and he gave everyone a sharp look of annoyance. His head tottered and his body swayed as if he was falling asleep. He dozed off; it was his usual nap time. He looked, though, as if he was hanging on for his last breath. And that ripped me apart. I held back tears and faced a whirlwind of nurses and doctors entering and exiting the room. It was nighttime by the time they settled him into a room. Then the nurses, who were wonderful, moved him to a workroom.

They proceeded to wash his face. I broke down watching this process, turning my head and hitting walls. While he was seated on a table, they washed his face in a saline solution and a handful of skin came off. He went crazy, hollering and screaming and reaching for me. I couldn't do anything for him. That killed me.

There was no way I was coaching a game on Thursday. It was the first round of the NCAA Tournament and I understood the significance for my program and alma mater. Yet how could I think of work with my son in the burn unit? How could I leave him? How could I leave my family? I didn't care if it was an historic event. It didn't feel as important as it had a day before. Nothing seemed as important as my son's health during those hours.

The burn unit supervisor, Dr. Sam Jones, told my wife and me it was too early to determine whether V.J. would need skin grafts or cosmetic surgery. That decision depended on the degree of his burns, which had not been determined. There were so many unknowns. I had to educate myself about skin grafts and cosmetic surgery. The process seemed too much for any baby. This only compounded my fears and made my choice to go to San Antonio harder.

V.J.'s full recovery would depend on how his face was treated. The nurses needed to wash his face carefully three times per day to avoid infecting his wounds. Each time they washed his face the treatment removed newly grown skin.

Watching this process took the life out of me because it was by far V.J.'s most painful experience. He cried the moment nurses walked in the door. I struggled watching him undergo this process and was determined to stay home. His cries filled me with such sorrow and I couldn't relieve his pain. I felt like a bad parent, even though I was present and engaged. What would it feel like to leave his bedside? How selfish could I be?

The situation made me question my priorities. Since childhood I had dreamed about going to the Division I NCAA Tournament, first as a player, then as a coach. And the opportunity had arrived. I lied to myself about the significance of the moment, hiding my real desire to participate in order to feel more like a caring father. Yet I was a caring father. That conundrum added more stress to an increasingly stressful situation. Who chooses a game over a sick child?

Dr. Jones decided V.J. should stay in the burn unit. Meanwhile, he encouraged me to go with the team to San Antonio. There was very little I could do for V.J., though that didn't make me feel comfortable because nothing had been settled. With it being so early in the process, the doctors provided few answers and we had no clear plan of action. I had to make a decision. I turned to my wife.

She told me, "You demand that your players remain tough, so you must practice what you preach and do the same." I agreed, though I couldn't escape my guilt. "You handle the team and the court and I'll handle the hospital and V.J.," she added.

I've never felt lower.

A Win for the Ages

Four days earlier, I had been riding the high of a lifetime. I was standing on a ladder, holding my son while I cut down a championship net cord inside Norfolk Scope Arena. Our team had won the

Mid-Eastern Athletic Conference men's championship game over Morgan State. We looked into the adoring crowd, filled with loved ones, friends and supporters, soaking in a surreal moment. Jet magazine captured the image shortly after. With that victory, our 20th in a row, we advanced to the men's Division I NCAA Tournament. We won the MEAC conference tournament for the first time since the 1950-51 season to earn an automatic berth into the championship, underscoring one of the best seasons in school history.

Our road to success started early in the season with an 82-72 upset victory over N.C. State, a traditional Atlantic Coast Conference powerhouse, on Nov. 20, 2013. That accomplishment, viewed in our region as a huge victory, put others on notice that we had an underdog squad with heart, skill, guile and toughness. We played as though we had something to prove.

And of course we had everything to prove, especially after falling short in the first round of the MEAC Tournament the season before. We had been top seeds picked to win it all and we had caved under the pressure.

So entering the 2013-14 season, our returning seniors – particularly point guard Emanuel Chapman, shooting guard Jeremy Ingram and forward Alfonzo Houston – were determined to get back to the tournament and make a run to the finals. They fed off my energy. I had learned from the previous season and prepared a pre-season training program harder than any I had installed during my five seasons as head coach. My team ran holes in their Nikes. We slowly morphed into form, fighting early-season injury.

At the end of the season, I was named MEAC coach of the year. Jeremy Ingram was named player of the year after averaging 20.6 points per game during the season and writing his name in the school's record books.

We entered the MEAC Tournament primed. In succession we defeated No. 8 seed Howard, 92-46; No. 4 seed Norfolk State, 68-

45 and No. 3 seed Morgan State, 71-62. That was the school's first basketball conference tournament championship in 64 years.

For two days, I floated on a natural high.

An Agonizing Decision

I'm generally a humble guy. However, alternating from such an incredible high to an extraordinary low put life in perspective. No parent wants to see an infant in the hospital. I love my job as coach at N.C. Central. But in 40 years, the school will likely have another coach and will continue educating student-athletes. My son only gets one father. So I hesitated to make the trip to San Antonio with the team, even as Dr. Jones gave his approval. I called our athletics director to apprise her of the situation.

There was a real chance that I might not coach the team in the NCAA Tournament.

Soon after, our chancellor, Dr. Debra Saunders-White, called my phone and left a message of prayer. Who does that? She won me over right there. Over time, others found out about V.J., and folks started texting, "Is V.J. okay?" Then phone calls poured in. While at the hospital on Tuesday night, I had a chance to think and talk with my wife about whether I would go with the team or stay with my son.

It came down to practicing what I preached. Throughout the season, I had asked my players to be tough, respond to adversity and make the next play. Damn it if I didn't have to apply those words to my own life. They looked to me for leadership and I had to look them in the eyes and answer their concerns. Do you take your own advice, coach?

I decided to take the trip.

Remaining in the hospital would have been just as painful. There was no safe haven. My wife gave me her blessing. She understood the moment and the man. I'm forever grateful to her for that example of unselfish love. I owe her even more than before.

She told me: "I'll take care of the hospital. You take care of the court."

Living with my Decision

Wednesday afternoon, on March 19, two hours before our chartered flight was scheduled to leave, I left the hospital, hoping to avoid the send-off celebration on campus. When I arrived, the camera crews were still waiting for me. I didn't want to talk to anyone, let alone fake enjoyment for a TV camera. I've never done that. I'm consistently myself, behind the scenes or in front for the news. I let reporters know that the day had turned bittersweet because of personal reasons.

They wanted to interview a coach. I just wanted to be a dad.

I broke the news to my team. I had missed several practices, an unusual occurrence for a team used to my hands-on approach. I wanted them to feel as normal as possible considering the bomb I dropped. Once we boarded the plane, I remember taking a seat next to Pastor Nate Davis, our team chaplain. I slept hard, waking at our destination.

We landed in San Antonio and the media was everywhere, making their way onto the bus at the hotel. My head spinning and my feelings displaced, I interviewed with WRAL's Jeff Gravley as soon as I arrived, trying to pull myself together. Inside the hotel, there were well-wishers with signs, noisemakers and pom-poms, perfect accessories for the occasion, though I just wanted to escape the fanfare. My heart and mind were miles away.

The next afternoon, reports about my son appeared on Twitter. I decided to officially inform the media at a scheduled press conference. If anyone was going to tell my story, it was going to be me. We are a private family, but I didn't want an accident turning into a fable and then into an ugly rumor. I didn't want someone talking about throwing hot grits on Al Green. Later, at the shoot around, I spoke with Marv Albert, the legendary television announcer who was assigned to our game for the NCAA Tournament, and he asked, "How's your son?" I couldn't escape the incident and that only made me worry more about V.J.

When I walked into my hotel room that evening, the situation fell on me like a hailstorm. The huge, beautiful suite felt so empty without my family. The room was fit for a queen, and my wife – the woman who had attended every high school game I coached, when we weren't even married yet – was not there to share the experience. Put me in a hole in the wall and I'm fine. The luxurious suites are for my wife, and she deserved to be there for that moment. Together we had worked to get to this grand stage, sacrificing time and plotting our path to such an achievement. This was her reward for all the support she had given over the years as I worked my way up the ranks from middle school coach to high school coach to college assistant to head college coach. It's not like my future had been written on the wall – like a gifted high school ballplayer – and there was a guarantee of anything. She had walked by faith with me to this pinnacle.

She's the one who helped throw a surprise party for me months before when I earned my master's degree in special education with a focus on learning disabilities. My wife always took care of the family and there she was again providing for my son.

I sat in my room and lounged in guilt. I started to compare myself to my father, who had walked out and never come back. It was an unfair comparison because the situations were so different, but the more you dwell on something the more tricks your mind plays. I stayed in my room most of the time in San Antonio. I passed on the festivities and kept the room dark.

I couldn't properly prepare for Iowa State, our opponent in the second round of the tournament. Befuddled by the turn of events,

I snapped on my team at practice, riding them unnecessarily. Aware of my mistake, I called them into my room and apologized for the poor treatment. I held so much respect for each player after the way they had progressed during the season. I wanted them to know I loved them.

My emotions swirled and spiraled and stretched and spun inside my body. I thank God there were no reckless moments because I was cocked and ready to fight over any indiscretion. The hardest job on the planet is that of a parent. I was useless to my child when he needed me most, and I had voluntarily left him to travel miles away. I couldn't shake the guilt.

CHAPTER 1

FATHERLESS

"He's gone ... And he ain't coming back."
Hattie McDougald

I don't remember much about when I was four years old, but I recall the night my father left the family as clearly as if it were a motion picture. That night, there was a rent party at my parents' apartment in the Orchard Park Houses in Boston. We lived in a two-bedroom apartment in public housing, nestled in a neighborhood considered one of the most notoriously dangerous in America in 1978.

Rent parties were common to families who lived at Orchard Park. After paying the host at the door, people gathered in a particular apartment to play records – then-called 45s – and danced well into the night. Guests devoured food and drank merrily, as if it were Christmas. The host collected money to help pay the rent. These spread around our neighborhood, supplementing meager incomes and providing much-needed entertainment for adults.

I hated these parties because I shared a small bedroom with my older brother Earl Moton, who we called Verne. When guests arrived, we had to share our room and toys with other kids in a tight space. On that night, it seemed like there were 30 kids crammed in there. I don't remember much about our room, except that a long row of black beads hung from my door and rattled every time someone entered.

I remember my pops coming into the room and taking orders from all the kids. "What do you want?" he said. Penny candy? Bubble gum? Soda? He took our orders, including my grape Now & Laters and walked out.

I never saw him again.

But I was waiting on my Now & Laters. *When is he going to bring those back?* One hour became two. Two hours became three. I fell asleep. He wasn't there the next day. I didn't know what to think. There were selfish thoughts about candy, and then I realized my father had not come home. Was he ever coming back? I soon learned he wasn't. "He's gone ... and he's not coming back," my mother, Hattie McDougald, said. She broke it down without emotion, careful not to stir too many feelings in us.

She couldn't show weakness because that might upset my brother and me. She didn't want us to assume the male role in the house, knowing we weren't ready for that. My brother was just five years older than I was. No matter how painful it was, my mother gave us the news straight. There was no sugar-coating. "Don't be lookin' for this guy to come back no time soon," she said. "He ain't coming."

This was startling news for a four-year-old. Of course I cried. Yet my mother never allowed us to use my father's departure as a crutch. She seemed callous and cold in her delivery, pulling us close and giving us the truth. Truth hurts, I found out early, but truth builds trust. My mother was committed to it. "We're going to look each other in the face, and we're going to be honest with each other," she said all the time. And that was it. I fell in line with her orders. I began to build a wall to shield me from the loss of my father, and eventually I didn't want him to come back. His absence, in a small way, was motivation. Bolstered by my mother's strength, I grew stronger, but I couldn't escape the deep, painful feelings I held inside. I grew a tough skin, thinking that one day I'd be able to say, "Dad, I did it without you."

On my fifth birthday, my father left a bike at my door. For weeks I had talked about getting a bike for my birthday. I believe my mother communicated this to my father. That only seems right, considering our birthday is on the same day. My mother was born June 16, 1947, and I was born June 16, 1974. We were even born at the same time: 5:06 a.m.

Without knocking or checking in, my father left this beautiful bike with a bow attached and a note with my nickname, Puffy.

I wanted to hop on that bike and ride around the neighborhood. But I resented my father for once again playing me for a fool – coming to our door but leaving again. I couldn't remember what he looked like. I thought if I rode that bike I would be accepting him leaving the way he had. So I never rode it. Believe me, it took a lot of willpower to stay off it, because I didn't have another bike.

I learned to make it without my father. My mother became both mother and father; I still give her Mother's Day and Father's Day cards. Still, I yearned to know more about my pops.

Losing your father has a greater effect on you than anyone knows. When my father left, I developed self-hatred. I felt I wasn't good enough. Kids gain confidence from their fathers. Many think of their father as Superman. They argue on the school bus about whose daddy is stronger. "My daddy's muscles are this big," they say.

I remember in the third grade people asking where my dad was. I lied: He's in Vietnam. Whatever popped into my mind. I'm forced to concoct grander and grander stories, and I soon grew tired of lying.

I walk around thinking: *If I wasn't appealing to my daddy, I don't expect to be appealing to you.* Girls make me uncomfortable. I spend a lot of time alone. My brother, who is older and finding his own way, is like, "Don't use my brush." He's living in another world. My lack of confidence turns into behavioral problems. We're not built to figure ourselves out at such a young age.

One day, I ask my mother about my father and her anger lets me know not to ask anymore. That subject is taboo. I'm dealing with the pain of my father not being there; meanwhile, she's dealing with the pain of her man not being present. Everyone in the family feels pain, but no one is communicating. His absence creates so many disadvantages in the family structure. I walk around pissed off.

In the early 80s, we moved from the Orchard Park projects to the Lane Street projects in Raleigh, N.C., trading one ghetto for another. My mother, who was raised in Dunn, N.C., moved us to the same Raleigh neighborhood as my grandmother, Mattie McDougald. My grandmother and I connected like cookies and milk. She was a Bible-loving, church-going woman who taught me everything from reading to multiplication. Heaping love on me, she helped me adjust and almost forget we were poor and fatherless.

I joined the Raleigh Boys & Girls Club and was introduced to organized sports. I joined a baseball team and immediately the absence of my father became more apparent. My mother had been an athlete, and she was as competitive as any male, yet she lacked instincts where sports were concerned. She wasn't adept at throwing, catching and hitting but she learned. Baseball was her first crash course. Coaches pitched to batters in the first league I joined. I knocked out more home runs than Reggie Jackson on that first team. Boys & Girls coach Ron Williams moved me to another team where batters faced pitching machines. At the next level, I struggled. I struck out four times in my first game. Prideful and embarrassed, I cried all the way home. To help me, my mother made my brother pitch to me as hard as he could while she played the outfield. We stayed out there all night until I started making contact. My mother threw the ball all over the place. She didn't know the difference between a proper batting stance and a karate stance. That was supposed to be my father in the field catching fly balls and making sure my feet were pointed in the right direction.

Throughout the projects in Boston and Raleigh there were so many kids who didn't have fathers that it almost felt bad to miss yours. If you knocked at a hundred doors, there wouldn't be a single father who answered the door. There were males, though most likely a boyfriend or brother but never a biological father. For the most part, we went on with our lives without dads, playing tough, secretly desiring their presence. It bothered me more than I let on.

My emotions would surface when other kids' fathers picked them up and took them somewhere, usually a ballgame or event. Back in Boston, we'd play football in the street and someone's dad would drive up the block and disrupt the game. He'd yell for his son to get in the car. "Where you going?" I'd ask. "To the game," he'd reply. That meant either the Boston Celtics or the Boston Red Sox. From the top floor apartment of our projects, you could see the downtown skyline, as well as the Boston Garden, home of the Celtics basketball team. As close as I lived to it, I had never visited the Garden.

I hated those surprise visits. They ended with me standing alone in the street and my friend waving from the back seat. The next day my friend returned with toys and stories about the game. That tortured me.

My dad's absence bothered me, and there were times when I couldn't avoid thinking of him. I remember March 1, 1986, as clearly as a bad dream. I was 11 years old. I walked into our two-bedroom apartment on Jones Street in Raleigh, and I thought someone had broken into the place. The door was cracked, and I heard crying. I walked into my mom's room, and she was on the floor sobbing uncontrollably. I had never seen her so dispirited, and it drove me berserk. I crawled on the floor and held my mom. Not once did I ask what was wrong or what was going on, because I knew there could be only one thing that could drive her to that emotional state.

Holding my mom's back and crying, I realized my grandmother had died. My grandmother had been back and forth to the hospital for months battling cancer. My mom was staying with her and caring for her in a house not far from our apartment. Mom was the youngest child and was attached to my grandmother's hip. I will never forget the ferocity of her crying and the sadness that overtook that dark room. We stayed on that floor all night.

My mother was distraught for weeks. As she mourned, she wept and barely slept. She broke down cooking dinner. My grandmother's death took an emotional toll I was in no way prepared to handle. My resentment toward my father turned to hatred. I remember thinking, "This is not my job." He should have been there to console my mother. He should have been with his family.

My grandmother's death and my father's absence started to affect me psychologically. If something happened to my mother, who would take care of me? I had a large family but they were estranged from my side of the family. I was scared of becoming an orphan and having to live in a strange place with strange people. If my mother stayed out later than midnight with her friends, I was quick to take her phone book and start dialing numbers. I was terrified of something happening to her. I couldn't exactly pick up the phone and call my father and that really bothered me.

I had almost hit puberty, and I was starting to understand more about the world. My behavior reflected my environment. I found father figures around the projects, a four-block radius filled with hustlers and customers. These guys were not appropriate father figures. From ages 12 to 16, I went through a thug stage. I started acting like the men I was around.

One day when I was on the playground with a friend, a pimp came up to us and asked, "Anybody seen my bitch running through here?" We looked at each other and said, "No, we haven't seen her." Several months later, in my first relationship, I got mad and called my girlfriend a "bitch." She quickly fired back, "You are not going to treat me like that." She was right. That wasn't appropriate, but I had never had a conversation with my father about how a man is supposed to treat and respect a woman. He had never taught me what to say, so I filled my mouth with the language of the street. I was on my own.

Life grew very frustrating. I survived with the help of a few good men. Coach Ron Williams at the Boys & Girls Club helped close some of the learning gaps. He was a hard-nosed guy who had played football at N.C. Central University. He set a standard for me to reach and never relented until I jumped high enough to clear the mark. My godfather, Slick, was a hustler but he steered me away from the streets. He taught me how to spot trouble and move to the other side of the block. Neighborhood baseball coach Peter Cheeks – a loud-talking, numbers-crunching businessman – taught me to stand up for what was right and use my gifts – in sports or school – to win the game. My high school basketball coach, Frank Williams, put his foot in my back and wrapped his arm around my shoulder, teaching me to walk as a young man.

Still, there was no replacing the father who had walked out on me. My mother was correct when she said he wasn't coming back.

After much contemplation, I turned that disappointment into motivation. Sports provided an outlet and helped me create an alter ego to get through the challenging years. My family remained poor through my middle and high school years. Working as a domestic, my mother held two jobs to provide for the family, stretching herself to the point of exhaustion. I excelled at basketball in high school, becoming an honorable mention McDonald's All-American.

I received offers from numerous schools, including N.C. State and Wake Forest and decided to attend N.C. Central University, where I am now the head coach. During my senior season there, I received a letter from my father.

The envelope came addressed to me in the coach's office. I read where it was from, a return address in Boston. At first, it didn't make sense. There were a couple of pages. In one passage he wrote that he hoped I was well. "Just wanted to say I'm sorry," it read. I refolded that letter, carried it to the post office and wrote "return to sender" on the envelope. I never told my mother. I knew what she thought about the dude: He was a loser. I didn't want to ruin my senior season with a messy reunion with a guy who had deserted us. He didn't deserve to share in my good fortune. Things were going really well for me. I was scheduled to graduate from college – as my brother had done – and I was the leading scorer in the Central Intercollegiate Athletic Association. I held dreams of reaching the NBA, and a few scouts had been to my games.

The season before, I had been named CIAA player of the year. I was featured on the cover of Dick Vitale's magazine, and newspaper articles were circulating about my feats. This was a mighty convenient time for my father to send a letter and try to reinstate himself in my life.

I was so angry with him, so full of hatred and hurt that I could not think beyond my feelings. I should have given him an opportunity to explain, but I could think only of negative things to say to him.

My thoughts returned to the years he missed. Where was he when we were living in the projects? Every day I'd walk home, and it was life and death on the streets. My route was littered with so many cats who were up to no good. We were living in undesirable circumstances, fending for ourselves with little resources. Many people and songs glorify the ghetto, proclaiming its beauty and wonder. Those who grow up in the ghetto want nothing to do with that description. They want out. There's nothing appealing about broken wine bottles and winos, crack houses and crack whores, murders and funerals. I watched my mother struggle to find financial stability. We used food stamps. We ate spam. There were days I couldn't fix my mouth to ask for a quarter, much less a dollar. My brother and I took turns walking to the public assistance office for government cheese. Things might have been the same – or even worse – if my father had been there, but at least he would have been there going through it with us. When that letter arrived, I couldn't see through the pain and hurt clearly enough to give him an opportunity to explain. So, yeah, I mailed it back.

I never heard from my father again.

I learned to live without my father, and I believed I could handle any situation. Then one day my 3-year-old daughter Brooke landed an unexpected punch through my defenses. Dropped off after a weekend at grandma's house, she ran into our house, crying, and clasped her arms around my knees.

"I want a new MeMa," she said of her grandmother. "She wouldn't let me ride that bike."

"Why," I asked, interrupted by my mother, who was trailing my daughter.

"I don't care about you telling on me," my mother said. "Go ahead and ask him why you can't ride that bike."

I cut a glance at my mother and her expression said, "Yeah, I'm talking about that bike."

Caught off guard, I had to regroup before kneeling down to explain why my daughter couldn't ride the rusty bike in my mom's shed. It was truly a Huxtable moment. Click on the television to "The Cosby Show" and replace Bill Cosby with me. I explained that no member of the Moton family would ever ride that bike. I emphasized that her daddy was not like my daddy; I wasn't going anywhere. I couldn't believe I was having that conversation with my child.

I fumbled through an explanation about my father leaving and then coming back to deliver a sky-blue bike. My daughter is inquisitive, and she put together that my father was connected to her grandmother, like I was connected to her mother. Then she asked, "Why did your dad leave?" That hurt.

I had kept that bike for 35 years, and it had turned a wood-like color. The birthday bow was still attached. The frame was rusty and dirty. I kept the bike as memorabilia. I'm strange that way. It was the only artifact I had of my father besides a worn picture. I didn't have much to remember him by, so that old bike served as a reminder of the man they say looks just like me. It wasn't in shape for anyone to ride. It was something dear to me because my father had given it to me, and no matter the circumstances, you want to love a gift from your father. Yet it was a reminder of the damage my father had done to my family.

I must prepare myself to have this conversation again with my daughter. She is full of questions and will no doubt pass information to her brother. Sadly, they will never know their grandfather and will have only melancholy, passed-down stories about him.

As for that rusty bike, I finally tossed it in the trash.

INSIDE THE

LOCKER ROOM

I often ask people, "What hurts more: never knowing your father or having him leave?" I'm convinced knowing your dad and having him walk out hurts more, if only a little more. I say this because I am a father now. My daughter Brooke, is now five years old and my son, LeVelle, Jr., is one. They will never know their grandfather. My father was Haitian, born in Port-au-Prince. That's all I know. I've never really pressed the issue with my mother. It's unfair to me, but I'm going to take that hit because I've seen her take harder hits for me.

There's something that should be respected, and a baton that should be passed from generation to generation so kids can understand the people they came from. That's in an ideal world.

Someone recently came up to me and said, "If you were a girl, you would have perfect eyebrows." She went on to ask, "Where are you from?" I told her Raleigh. She protested, "No, do you have some family member from somewhere else or something because women pay money every week to get their eyebrows like that." I was like, "Wow." I told her my father was Haitian. She said,

"That's what it is." When I posted a picture of my daughter on Facebook, someone said, "Her eyebrows are perfect." My wife Bridget responded, "Well, you should see her father's." Now I've never paid close attention to anyone's eyebrows, but I had to admit to myself, "I get my eyebrows from him." And then I start to question what else I got from my father.

But more than anything, I just want a relationship. At 39, I would take that right now however it came. I'm not sure it will ever happen, but I'm ready to participate.

It's taken a long time to get here. I grew into a successful adult without knowing my father. I did not use the fact that my father was not in my life as an excuse, not for anything. I never used it as a crutch. That's what got me through, relying on my inner strength and using my anger as fuel to motivate me. I relied on the support that was available, especially from my mother, who never allowed me to make an excuse.

If you want to move on and heal, you have to forgive. I don't think you can ever really forget. And I don't think you ever stop crying. I still have moments when I just go off and I've got to let it out. My wife has never seen it. My mom has never seen it. That's just my moment of grieving. I can be in the car and I'll feel tears roll down my cheeks.

Yes, I finally forgave my dad for not being in my life. My ability to forgive came much later in my adulthood, but I had to free myself. I couldn't hold the hatred in my heart any longer.

I couldn't take it personally anymore. That was my mistake. I took my father's decision to leave as a personal assault for so many years, creating a void in my life I never filled. My father was an adult, and he made an adult decision. He has to live with that decision. I didn't understand that at the time. But I understood that I didn't have to be a failure because of his choice.

That was so important for me to realize. My peers often internalized their failures based on their parents' bad decisions or their brothers' actions. Some would say, "My brother went to jail, so I'll probably go to jail, too." They said this as if there were no alternatives. I avoided following a path of self-destruction simply because my father chose not to remain in our household. Armed with education and willpower, I learned to make better decisions regarding family.

You are capable of success regardless of any adult's choice to be in your life. If you live with your mother, place your trust in your mother. Trust and pray she has the strength to carry the family through. Single mothers are strong but not invincible. Make her job easier by doing your part. My mother taught me to be tough in the face of adversity. She frowned upon moping and sulking, even if it was my father I was crying over. "Pull it together," she would say.

If you're living without a father, I've walked in your shoes. I know it's not easy. Some days are rougher than others. The world is a hard place. There must be something spiritual that gets you through. The thing that carried me through was my relationship with God. The rest is smoke and mirrors. Your job is to survive and grow. You pray, survive, and grow into a healthy adult. Carrying hatred for someone else's bad decision is unhealthy.

CHALKBOARD

1. Forgiveness: Forgiveness is the most important step in the healing process. As a kid, I saw the world in black and white, right and wrong. There was no gray area. If you were for me, I loved you, and if you were against me, I couldn't stand you. This perspective made me build up a furious hate for my father. I burned through years hating my father, and I was the person hurt in the exchange. I grew weary and tired. That much hate and anger drains your spirit. It took a while, but I realized the only person my anger was truly affecting was me. I was under the impression I had forgiven him a long time ago, but I had only excused him. I first had to forgive myself, and then I had to learn to forgive him. Once that was complete, I had to let it go and release the negative energy that had consumed my mind since the day he left. I accepted that the pain of my past could hinder my future, and I didn't want to block future blessings by not forgiving. So I did. My time and my life are too valuable to wallow in the misery of yesterday. A weight has been lifted off my shoulders, and peace of mind has entered my life because I chose to forgive. If God forgives, then so can we.

2. It's NOT Your Fault: For years, I held myself responsible for my father leaving. It was as if things were fine until I came along, and then all of a sudden, he was gone! Was I the cause of him leaving? Did he love me? Was he ashamed of me? Those questions left me with no closure. Then one day I realized his choice to leave wasn't about me. It was about him. You don't get to choose your parents, and you're definitely not responsible for their actions. Blaming yourself places you in an unfair equation of responsibility that you're not accountable for. Maybe he couldn't be the man in my life because he was still a boy. For whatever reason, it was about him and not about me.

3. Find a Father Figure: There's a reason it takes two people to create a child: It takes two people to raise one. I believe that every fatherless child seeks out a father figure. I strongly encourage you to find one who's positive. This is vital for your growth and development into a man. My mother did an outstanding job of raising me and instilling in me what she thought a man should do, but I was constantly searching for a male figure who could teach me what a man should do. Fortunately, I found that in Ron Williams at the Boys & Girls Club, and Peter Cheeks, who owned a fashion design company and sponsored a local baseball team. Both took the time to provide male nurturing for me and other kids without fathers. I can't say I sought them out as mentors, but I put myself in position to receive guidance. I can't say that anyone filled the role of father in my life, though I know these men offered me the time, advice and love that fathers can provide. They were influential in my development and key, along with my mother, in shaping my self worth.

Take advantage of programs at schools, libraries, churches or community centers that offer mentoring. Ask your guidance counselor about programs such as Big Brothers Big Sisters. I've found that people who find positive mentors involve themselves in activities they enjoy. Volunteers are willing to share their time and experience in activities beyond sports. Actively pursue opportunities and a mentor may present himself to you. Soon you will discover that anyone can be a father, but it takes a special someone to be a dad.

CHAPTER

2

NEW EDITION

"You can't connect the dots looking forward. You can only connect them looking backwards. So you have to trust that somehow your dots will connect in the future. You have to trust in something. Your gut, destiny, life, karma, whatever. This approach has never let me down, and it has made all the difference in my life."
Steve Jobs, co-founder of Apple, Inc.

New Edition saved my life.

It sounds funny when I say that out loud, and so many people have looked at me crazy when I've said it, but I'm serious. Bobby Brown, Ronnie DeVoe, Ralph Tresvant, Michael Bivins and Ricky Bell inspired me to make something of myself. Their success as New Edition convinced me that I too could make it out of the ghetto.

They grew up in Boston, where I'm from. Most people associate the city with the Boston Tea Party, Paul Revere, the American Revolution, Harvard Square or sports teams such as the Celtics, Patriots and Red Sox. There are other landmarks and areas less familiar, including Roxbury, where I was born. My family stayed in a housing project called Orchard Park, also known as OPP or The Bricks.

Members of New Edition also lived in Orchard Park. I knew them before they released the album "Candy Girl" in 1983 and became world famous. Back then, they were teenagers, older than me by five or six years. We weren't friends, but my mamma knew their mammas, and my brother knew their friends, just as we knew other families in the projects. We'd see them on the street and speak. They attended the local high school.

Some viewed our neighborhood as Vietnam because of the high homicide rates, gang activity, excessive drug traffic, crime and violence. With an average income of about $9,000 per household in 1974, the area was ranked as poor, with many families living below the poverty line. Such rampant poverty created a ghetto wild, wild West environment, where merely walking out of the house required you to have your head on a swivel. Your 21st birthday wasn't promised; in fact, it was a far-fetched proposition. As a kid, you'd witness others becoming products of their environment, dying in the streets. So many succumbed to the negativity of our surroundings. They got involved in illegal activity and chose a life of crime because they figured there wasn't much reason to live.

I thank God that He gave me vision beyond my circumstances. Though my environment reeked of dysfunction and was a place where "hurt people hurt people" and "broken people break people," I had faith that I would escape that war zone and become something. As a child, you know right from wrong, and my environment felt wrong. I didn't have the slightest clue how I would escape or what I might become, but I believed in God, even at six years old.

Eventually, He showed me my path out in the form of New Edition.

New Edition members were my neighbors. Ralph and Ricky lived on Adams Street in the apartment building next to mine. Bobby lived nearby on Eustis Street, and Mike lived across the projects on Tan Court. Ronnie lived across town in Cathedral

Projects. His uncle, Brooke Payne, a local dance legend, became the group's choreographer.

That's how it started for them. Payne named the guys New Edition, a nod to The Jackson 5, the progenitors of boy bands such as New Kids on the Block, NSYNC and the Backstreet Boys that rocked the 80s, 90s and 2000s. Under Payne's direction, New Edition practiced like the Celtics, rehearsing long hours to master intricate routines that required talent and athleticism. A visionary and taskmaster, Payne cracked the whip. And it worked.

In 1982, the group was ready when it entered the local Hollywood Talent Night at Strand Theatre. Maurice Starr, a local singer and producer, was offering $500 and a recording contract to the winner. New Edition took second place, impressing Starr enough to earn an invitation to record its first album. The guys put out "Candy Girl" in 1983, and the news rang out through the neighborhood, especially after the album's title track became a smash on local radio and eventually climbed to No. 1 on the national charts. Yet they were still living in the projects with us.

This was pre-Internet, before there were YouTube videos to validate stardom. It was rare to find a household with cable television. There was no easy way to know how popular these guys were. I'd ask myself, "Why are they wearing the same bargain clothing as everyone else?" How could they be stars living in Apartment 5E?

And then we saw them.

"Velle, Velle," my mother shouted. "Come here. Hurry. You gotta see this."

When I sprinted into the living room, I couldn't believe my eyes. Ralph, Bobby, Ronnie, Ricky and Mike were on "Soul Train," dancing and singing "Candy Girl." My mother turned up the volume. We looked at each other as if to say, "This is amazing." In the African-American community, "Soul Train" solidified your celebrity. There were no more doubts.

We watched them, dignified in white sequined shirts, white pants and white patent leather shoes, dancing as if they had no bones. New Edition was on TV with soul brother number one, "Soul Train" host Don Cornelius. They were stars.

That moment changed my life. Five guys from the same ghetto, the same dysfunction, had not only escaped Orchard Park but made it onto national television. Chills ran through my body and goose bumps formed on my skin as I danced and sang with the group.

Up to that point, I hadn't seen any kids who looked like me on television. We watched "Diff'rent Strokes" but the black characters, Willis and Arnold, weren't dressed like us. They were too straight-laced. When I saw Ralph in the streets, he was wearing Kung Fu outfits, popular at the time. Bobby was a DJ and hosted block parties. We laughed at "Diff'rent Strokes," but it wasn't anything like our lives. There certainly wasn't any rich white man looking to rescue us from the projects and shepherd us to Park Avenue.

Once New Edition's television performance ended, I ran to the playground, where the projects seemed to buzz with talk about the group. Everyone was discussing them, even the hardest of the hard gangsters. I had an incredible idea that I thought would serve as my escape from the projects. I knocked on the door of four of my friends and told them we were going to be the next New Edition. We would follow the blueprint laid by our heroes. We would sing, recite and mimic their every dance move.

Rehearsals would begin the next day, and we wanted to be better than New Edition. We expected to sign a record deal. All of this was sure to happen, but under one condition: I got to be Ralph Tresvant. I was the lead singer and the group would have to accept that. Over time, group members disagreed with me being the lead and argued their point. Some wanted to fight. Pushes turned into shoves and shoves turned into fistfights. My first three fistfights were over "Who's gonna be Ralph?" My stubbornness prevailed.

I dismissed members and recruited others to replace them. For Christmas, my mother purchased a VCR and cable television service. To help me learn New Edition's routines, I recorded the group's performances on shows such as "Showtime at the Apollo," "American Bandstand" and "Solid Gold."

Other people had escaped Orchard Park. Donna Summer unveiled her talents and became a disco queen in the 1970s. The Nation of Islam leader Minister Louis Farrakhan was born in Roxbury in the 1930s and made a name as a Calypso singer before rising in the Black Muslim ranks. Basketball all-star Jimmy Walker was raised on the courts of Roxbury and was selected No. 1 overall in the 1967 NBA draft by the Detroit Pistons. Surely there were other successful folks from the region, but at that time, there was no one successful from my neighborhood who looked like me. New Edition members were regular dudes. They wore Wrangler jeans like me. Their hair was combed like mine; Ralph cut a long part and brushed waves into his hair. They had crooked teeth. I looked at them differently because they represented me.

The hit song "Candy Girl" was a reason to like them, yet I idolized them because they came from where I came from, a place most people despised and dismissed. We lived in Third World conditions you might find in Haiti, Afghanistan or Somalia. This was before the crack epidemic, yet there were daily shootings, stabbings, robberies, prostitution, poverty, low employment rates and general decay. Our apartment hallways smelled of urine, and inside, the walls were cardboard thin. Sitcoms joked about this type of disrepair and rot but to live among the blight and broken windows was not funny.

We were proud people but our living circumstances were reprehensible. My mother worked at the Gillette plant and made decent money. Working two jobs, she had saved and was close to moving us to the suburbs. Most of the time she traveled to her night job at Gillette with her best friend, Lola Rivera, but one evening she decided she wasn't going in because she had numerous vacation days and needed a rest. "I told her to just go into work and call when you get home," my mother said about Lola. "She lived a couple blocks from me, but that night she never did call."

It wasn't like Lola not to call. They usually traveled together by train and then bus to and from work. They would check in with each other once they were safe at home. This night, however, Lola walked out of the train station and was attacked by gang members while waiting for the bus home. They followed her from the station, and robbed and beat her for the purse she was carrying. When the gang members realized she had no money, they elevated their terror. One guy ran across the street to a filling station and retrieved a can of gasoline. They poured it over Lola's body and set her on fire. "All because she didn't have, in her purse, what they wanted her to have," my mother said. "Over nothing."

Lola was in the hospital for a week. She lived long enough to give detectives descriptions of her assailants. Her story ran on the evening news and in the newspaper, drawing sympathy from the neighborhood.

"If I had went to work that night," my mother said. "Oh my goodness. I would've probably been lying next to her."

Tired and scared, my mother decided she had had enough of Boston's frigid weather and hospitality. Many of her friends were moving back South and she thought the timing was right. We packed our bags for North Carolina, moving in with my grandmother before settling into a two-bedroom apartment on Jones Street in Southeast Raleigh. We moved from Orchard Park Houses to Lane Street projects, a few blocks from the Historic Oakwood district and the Governor's Mansion. Though she felt the move provided more safety, my mother essentially traded one ghetto for another, as Lane Street held the same vice and mischief as our old neighborhood.

We settled into our new home around the time New Edition released its self-titled album, and the single "Cool it Now" was a smash. My mother bought me the record, along with Michael Jackson's "Thriller" album, for Christmas. I wore out the record player spinning "New Edition," dancing in my living room to every song. I knew every word and memorized the steps to every routine. Studious and limber, I kept up with the group step-for-step, locking, spinning, kicking, flexing, bending, gyrating and singing at the same time. They were my guys from Boston.

I spent so many hours trying to master the group's routines that I had time for nothing else except school and sports. I stayed off the streets and immersed myself in the art of New Edition.

I loved when my mother went to work. When she left in the morning, and my brother was working, I had the house to myself. Our apartment was about the size of a classroom, but I made space for two activities: indoor basketball and New Edition routines. I would take laundry baskets and coordinate an ACC Tournament. I balled up a sock and had two laundry baskets as my goals, attaching them at opposite ends of the apartment. I knew the roster of every ACC team. I stacked games so that North Carolina would win. It was always UNC and N.C. State in the finals. I orchestrated the outcomes so that Michael Jordan hit the final shot.

When I took a break from basketball, I performed New Edition routines. I moved the living room furniture into the kitchen. I nearly broke the VCR rewinding so often. I studied the albums. I knew song lyrics as if I had written them. I knew what the inside of the album covers looked like, as well as who earned producer and songwriter credits. I was in North Carolina putting on a show. I knew I was going to form the next big group. No one could tell me different.

I had formed my own group and we were performing in local talent shows. The transition to North Carolina felt easy because my brother and I had spent summers there with my grandmother, making friends and playing with the neighborhood kids. I've always been a leader, so I took full control over my group. It's hilarious to think back on those days. I had convinced myself the world needed another New Edition and somehow my group would be discovered and our ticket punched for "Showtime at The Apollo." So we had to be ready.

My friends and I arrived early at the bus stop to practice our moves. Picture that: Five skinny kids lined up in front of invisible microphone stands, synchronized and smooth, dancing hard and singing their hearts out.

As the leader, my credibility was challenged. No one believed I knew the group. "I'm from Boston," I argued. "They grew up in Orchard Park. I used to see them all the time." In hindsight, the story does seem far-fetched. I heard it all the time: "You don't know no New Edition. Stop lying." And that's when we started rumbling.

More than fighting, we practiced. We entered every talent show in the region, building our repertoire. We were competitive. If a guy missed a step, we punished him by requiring him to rewind the tape to the start of a particular song. This was during the cassette tape era, when finding a song was like a medieval form of torture.

As a child, sports dominated my choices, but it wasn't just sports. I diversified. I thought that's what you had to do to make it. I didn't know which bus was going to take me out of the projects: the baseball bus, the basketball bus, the football bus or the dancing bus. I just wanted to get on a bus to somewhere. I formed quintets throughout middle school and into high school, always on the lookout for the bus out of the city.

By the time I arrived at Enloe High School in 1988, New Edition had broken up. Bobby Brown had left the group in 1986 to pursue a solo career. The other members remained and put out a new album, "Heart Break," in 1988, adding Johnny Gill. My group crushed the new material and won a few talent shows in the late 80s, but New

Edition started to fade during my sophomore year. Some members took a hiatus and others launched projects, including Bell Biv DeVoe, which soared like fireworks and sold millions of records. Ralph and Johnny starred as solo artists, releasing platinum-selling albums.

We structured our dance routines based on New Edition, but sang popular rhythm and blues songs in the 90s. We sang and danced in variety shows and entered a lip-syncing contest at Enloe; it was like "Showtime at The Apollo" at our high school. They sold tickets for Thursday and Friday night competitions, and people from other high schools would break their necks to get into them. If the show started at 7 p.m., there would be a line wrapped around the building at 5 p.m. First prize was $50. I had to go get that.

The ladies loved us because we were popular. Not fine but popular. We were freshmen and sophomores. Some of the older students would pay me $5 to help them with their New Edition routines. "What song are we doing?" I'd ask. "'You're Not My Kind of Girl?' Sure." Then I'd perform the steps from memory.

We were pretty good at the routines, and after a few wins in talent shows we gained confidence. I remember my homeboy telling me, "'Yo, man, if we make it, you have to decide what you're going to do: basketball or stay in this group?" I'm amused by this heart-to-heart conversation now, though then we were contemplating a future on the road, away from the ghetto.

In 1991, my junior year of high school, my cousin told me to come back to Boston for a weekend because Bell Biv DeVoe was shooting a video in Orchard Park called "Word to the Mutha!" I convinced my mother to let me go for a day.

When I arrived, the scene was chaotic. There were helicopters, police officers and guards securing the projects. The entire community was gathered. There were four guys who seemed out of place, dressed in denim. We all wondered who they were because they were nerdy and dressed like Urkel. They would become one of the greatest singing groups of all-time: Boyz II Men. Michael Bivins discovered them.

I wanted to speak with New Edition members to let them know what they meant to me. During a break in shooting, security let me into their trailers, where we joked about how surreal life was in that moment. I told them I lived in North Carolina and had flown in for the video shoot. We took pictures and one of our mutual friends, Travis, said, "You know Velle is one of the top basketball players in the country." They showed love, congratulated me and advised me to stay focused.

On my flight back to North Carolina, it dawned on me that New Edition had saved my life. Countless hours of rehearsal kept me off the streets. I applied that discipline on the basketball court and developed a drive to be great. My immersion into their world made me believe I mattered. It brought me closer to my dream of escaping poverty. Who would think five guys from Orchard Park dancing on "Soul Train" could make such an indelible mark?

INSIDE THE

LOCKER ROOM

I didn't know what I wanted to be when I was growing up. I just wanted something from life; I didn't want to be a statistic. I wanted to make my mamma proud. The world had already told us: "Dude, this is what you're going to be. Here are your options – bum in the park, drug dealer or a prisoner." That bleak picture is the toughest image a kid could see. New Edition inspired me to move with a purpose. They showed me their blueprint, and I copied aspects that suited me.

I am big believer of the Law of Attraction. I believe wholeheartedly that our thoughts, whether positive or negative, have a profound impact on our lives. Our thoughts and emotions act as spiritual magnets, and once we send them into the universe, they radiate, and we attract what the universe has to offer. Therefore we attract reflections of ourselves.

That makes the mind the greatest single tool a person possesses. I believe I was so passionate, ambitious and obsessed with becoming New Edition that I emitted positive vibes that shaped me into the person I am today. The power of my thoughts created relationships and coincidences that otherwise would not have occurred.

The model for my basketball teams always has been New Edition. You have six creative personalities with egos who achieved individual successes. However, despite their disagreements and solo accomplishments, they are at their best as one unit: New Edition. The total is greater than the sum of the parts. That's how I see my basketball team. Everyone on the roster has attained success individually, but it never works unless egos are checked for the greater good of the team.

New Edition and I have become very good friends. Every concert the group has in the area, the guys invite me and leave me backstage passes and tickets. They allowed me to fulfill a lifelong dream when I went onstage and rehearsed with them before a BET concert. If that wasn't enough, in 2008 they let me propose on stage to my girlfriend (now my wife) because they wanted to share that experience with me. So many people share similar stories.

Their pursuit of excellence – dancing and singing their hearts out before adoring fans – taught me persistence, discipline and dedication. While immersing myself in their world, I became a perfectionist, making sure every move I made popped with the same explosion the group presented. When I nailed a step perfectly, it was satisfying.

At first, even my mother doubted my seriousness. One morning I was singing and dancing in the kitchen, and she burst into the room, screaming for me to sit down. I didn't even know she was there. "I'm trying to sleep," she said. But after we won a couple of talent shows and I showed her videos of us winning, she changed her tune. A couple of years later, she burst into the room as she had before. This time, however, she screamed, "You're holding your notes too long. Breathe through your nose." My mother was a singing instructor that morning. We laughed a long time about that advice.

I transferred that discipline, persistence and dedication to sports and school activities. Emulating New Edition was risky. I could have listened to other kids and been discouraged. Instead, I listened to my internal voice. I've always been a leader and it made sense to follow New Edition's example. I encourage you to follow your instincts and look at entertainers with a careful eye. Listen to your favorite artist's music and watch your favorite football player score touchdowns, but understand how they gained success. Research their history. Read magazine articles. Watch television interviews. Study their work ethic. Search for methods beyond the surface style. Then ask yourself: How can I achieve better? If your idols set records, dream about breaking them. Remember, the Law of Attraction starts in the mind.

You are responsible for your own life. You create your reality. I'm glad I had New Edition to assist me.

CHALKBOARD

1. Take a Leap of Faith: Science says "Show me and I'll believe." Faith says, "Believe and I'll show you." You must take that leap into the unknown to find success, but that requires you to have faith and believe. Anything worthwhile I've done in my life initially scared me to death. However, I don't believe God put me on this earth to be average. You must get beyond fear; you must get beyond your present circumstances. Your thoughts can become words and your words can become actions, but first you must believe in yourself and visualize your dreams. Growth and change are painful, but there's nothing more painful than staying stuck someplace you don't belong.

2. Find a Positive Role Model: It's important that you identify someone you respect and adopt that person as a role model. You may pick more than one. But selecting someone, perhaps a professional athlete or a teacher at your school, will give you a model for skills that may affect your life. Look for someone who has skills you want to copy. Emulate until you find your voice.

3. Be Original: You were born an original, so don't die a copy. No one can be a better you than YOU! Study your idols to develop your voice. You can emulate them with practice, but eventually you will deviate from the script and find your own voice. Two coaches, Mike Krzyzewski of Duke and Roy Williams of UNC-Chapel Hill work approximately 10 miles from where I coach, and many consider them worthy of Mount Rushmore. I developed close relationships with both; I have attended their practices and discussed coaching philosophies. As great as they are, I can't be them. They've found their niches and their greatness because of their conviction in what they do. I believe in me, and I've found that the only thing that will allow me to follow in their footsteps is to be me!

CHAPTER

3

STRIKE THREE

*"Failures are a part of life. If you don't
fail, you will never learn. If you never
learn, you will never change."*
Unknown

Before my family settled in Raleigh, we vacationed there at my grandmother's home, when I was 5, in the summer of 1980. One afternoon while out driving, we passed the Boys & Girls Club and I spotted a youth baseball game. I begged my mother to stop. Wide-eyed and eager, I wanted to play with the other kids, who appeared to be my age. It was a sunny afternoon and the sky was a beautiful Carolina blue. Kids were hitting balls, throwing and catching in the grass. We stood and watched until Ron Williams, the director of programs at the club, invited me to join the others. And like a pop fly falling into an open glove, my love affair with baseball began.

We moved to Raleigh three years later, and I continued to play baseball. I started from scratch and quickly improved, grasping the fundamentals with precision. I had strong hand-eye coordination and that helped me advance. Baseball was the only sport my mother watched on television, and I took a real interest, captivated by the home runs, batting averages and game-to-game statistics. I've always been good with math, and I memorized players' stats. Over time, Ron moved me from tee-ball to machine pitch to fast pitch. By the time I was 9, I was playing on the 10- to 12-year-old teams. I batted left-handed but could switch-hit.

Swinging a bat is one of the most natural things I've ever done. I can't explain it, and I don't want to know why. It's a God-given talent. All I know is I can still hit a 92 mph fastball at the batting cage. I was even more skilled as a teenager.

As a kid, I felt as comfortable on a baseball diamond as I felt on a playground. I learned every position, though I was primarily a pitcher and catcher. Ron has reminded me that I was always first in line to try new techniques. "You gave it your all to learn how to play," he said.

Ralph Capps, who was the senior director of the club, also coached youth baseball. He recalled a play I made that sticks in his mind. "You were playing third base," he said, "and a guy hit a line drive; looked like it was gonna surely be down the line for extra bases. Just as those major leaguers do today, you just extended out and back-handed that ball and caught it. My goodness."

The Boys & Girls Club team nurtured my talents. My local team exploited them – in a good way. Two brothers, Ralph and Roddley Redd, were coaches of the Pine State team, which played in the Lions Park league. Players from around the state played in this league and the skill level was high. Teams picked up new players through a draft.

Ralph and Roddley Redd were always on the lookout for new talent. They had watched me during club games and convinced me to throw the draft so they could select me for their team. I wasn't quite sure why they wanted me to play poorly, but I started to understand when coaches overlooked me. There was an order to the way teams chose players, and Ralph and Roddley Redd wanted me. So per their instructions, I acted as though I was a fumbling, bumbling neophyte during tryouts. I allowed balls to skid under my glove and go between my legs. I swung wildly at pitches, feigning fear, and shook my head as I purposely missed bunts. I made it appear as though I was the worst player on the field. Everyone knew I was the youngest, so they fell for the ruse.

Their plan worked. No coach wanted me, except, of course, Ralph and Roddley Redd, who had a perfect three spot in the rotation for me. In our first game, I came out swinging and making contact, which seemed like a miracle to the coaches who had watched me blow routine plays and flail at easy-to-hit, over-the-plate pitches. It was the ultimate hustle.

The youngest kid on the team stunned the league with a mean glove and a booming bat, and my ego certainly gained from the experience.

My name started to get out and, as a result, I started acting cocky. I became a sunglasses-wearing, pager-carrying, here-are-some-tickets-to-my-game star. I posed for pictures, too. My neighborhood started to notice after word got back that "Lil' Velle" could play. Our team was winning and that spread the word even faster and farther.

In less than half a season, I had found my niche and thought I had earned my stripes. My confidence was sky-high, like a successful major leaguer. Watching television and reading magazines, I emulated the professionals down to their stances. Now when I walked to the plate, I chewed Bubblicious and blew bubbles. I drew lines under my eyes to block the sun, and I stuffed batting gloves in my back pocket. I never rushed, taking my time outside the batter's box. I came to the ballpark in full character.

Batting lefty, I had swag like Tim Raines, extending the bat behind me when I made contact. Behind the plate as catcher, I mimicked Carlton Fisk, catcher's mask pulled to my forehead, a sweatband on my wrist, and a hand on my hip. At shortstop, it was all Ozzie Smith; I was smooth with my delivery to first. And on base, I was Rickey Henderson, taking huge leads for steals. They couldn't tell me nothing.

Our team rolled. We marched through the regular season and playoffs, and reached the championship game, where we faced Method. The stands were packed. By the third inning, we trailed 4-2, and it was my turn up at the plate.

I smashed a two-run triple, bringing two runs home and tying the game 4-4. It was my second hit of the day. I remember the stadium looking like Fenway Park – home of my beloved Boston Red Sox – teeming with people clapping and cheering.

Later, Method scored a go-ahead run and took a 5-4 lead. The game came down to the last inning and my final at-bat. It was the moment I had been waiting on all season. With my team down by one run, I walked to the plate with the bases loaded.

I was confident – perhaps a little too confident. I had studied Method's pitcher, Wilbert Hunter, from the dugout and he seemed to be losing control. His pitches were all over the strike zone. Somehow, though, I knew he would collect himself, find his rhythm and throw strikes when I arrived at the plate. He was a really good pitcher.

Standing at the plate, I envisioned a glorious outcome. I was prepared to be the hero. My teammates counted on me to make contact. I intended to hit that ball hard and far. I knew Hunter was going to throw strikes down the middle. He put heat on his pitches and depended on the fastball.

He threw two strikes and I fouled off both. Then he threw three balls. Facing a full count, I took a timeout and stepped out of the batter's box. It was the moment you dream about as a baseball player, the ultimate scenario: You smash a full-count home run and trot around the bases a hero, teammates surrounding you in euphoria at home plate. Game over.

You never dream about swinging and missing. But that's what I did. I looked head-on at a strike down the middle and whiffed, ending the game for my team by striking out. Ouch.

I can't explain how I missed that pitch. He threw a perfect strike down the middle, the kind you wish for, the kind you tee-off on and pound out of the stadium. Not me. I missed. I failed.

Daunted, I collapsed at home plate. Method's team celebrated around me, kicking dirt in my mouth. From the stands, my brother looked at me in disbelief. For once that season, I felt like the youngest player on the team. I wanted to cry. I wanted my mother. I wanted to get out of there as fast as possible. There was no way to make the situation right. There are no do-overs to change the course of history.

Afterward, there was an awards ceremony. Second-place medals were draped around our necks. I took mine off. Later, I threw it in the creek, copying Muhammad Ali, who had tossed his Olympic gold medal. I had just let my team down, and I didn't want to be rewarded. I couldn't stomach the loss. I thought I heard kids saying, "That dude's a loser." My mind was playing tricks on me. The older guys on the team looked at me as though we had all chipped in for a winning lottery ticket and I had lost it.

To make matters worse, my brother laughed at me. That fool laughed at my failure. It might as well have been my funeral. He had stuck the knife into a wound that was gushing like a geyser. I was in serious pain by the time I got home.

My mother tried to console me, saying, "It ain't the end of the world." She wasn't that great at pity parties. She'd hug you, but you had about 10 minutes of fluffy affection and then it was on to the next problem.

The next day there was a story in the paper explaining how we lost, which proved to me that it was the end of the world. I walked into the Boys & Girls Club and everyone was talking about the game. I love Ron Williams to death, but even he was harsh in his assessment. It was devastating to hear the disappointment in everyone's voices, especially as they were trying to make me feel better. I only felt embarrassment.

Our team had scored five runs in that game, and I had brought in three of them. I hit a two-run triple. I was nine, the youngest guy on the team. It didn't matter. I will recall that final at-bat for the rest of my life.

"Strike three," the umpire said. "You're out."

INSIDE THE

LOCKER ROOM

That final at bat remains in my mind as if it happened 15 minutes ago. It's a fresh wound some days. It was embarrassing, humiliating and tragic. I had let my team down and failed to deliver on the biggest stage when the world was watching. My friend and teammate on that squad, Greg McNeil, reminds me of that strikeout every time he sees me, even 30 years later.

Still I've never let that one disappointment define me. I didn't allow failure to become a string of failures and excuses. Fortunately, I am an avid reader. If you walk into my office, you immediately notice my book collection. I've chosen books by successful people from different walks of life, races and creeds, from Steve Jobs to Sean "Puffy" Combs. From Bill Gates to Walt Disney. Their stories and occupations are different, but they have a common denominator: There was a time when each failed, and failed miserably. They had felt the same humiliation and embarrassment I felt.

Those books taught me that failure is inevitable. It doesn't matter if you're Steve Jobs; you can be fired from a company you founded. It doesn't matter if you're

Puffy Combs; you can be fired from Uptown Records,
a company you helped build. It doesn't matter if you're
Michael Jordan; you can miss 33 game-winning shots.
These successful individuals taught me that failure is
only a stepping stone to success. Don't be afraid.

I'm a product of an environment where others were
more talented, more gifted, but the moment they failed,
they refused to try again. They never realized how close
they were to success when they gave up. I was once told
that every test in our life makes us bitter or better. Every
problem comes to break us or make us. The choice is
ours whether we become victims or victors. Remember,
you must go through to get through. And you must get
through to get to.

CHALKBOARD

1. Own It: When failure occurs, it's important to learn from the situation. That lesson begins and ends with you, as Michael Jackson would sing, "the man in the mirror." Have an honest conversation with yourself. The ability to look in the mirror and own your mistake is critical for growth beyond your circumstances. I've seen people blame the weather, their friends, co-workers, teammates, referees and anyone else so they can to avoid taking responsibility for their failures. As a result, they remain stuck.

Some people never discover the true lesson because they are constantly looking to deflect blame. That strikeout occurred when I was 9 years old, but it forced me to look in the mirror and have an honest conversation about what I didn't do. I could have blamed my teammates, the bat, the umpire and the ball, though I blamed myself.

I didn't keep my eye on the ball through contact. That was something I was taught from day one. Therefore I struck out. That type of personal accountability has taken me through life. It's allowed me to be successful in situations where the world doubted me.

That type of honesty carried me solidly into manhood. I didn't have a clue about how to be a coach, a father, a husband or a man, but I knew they all began and ended with owning mistakes. You will never read an article or watch an interview about our N.C. Central team where we lose a game and I blame anyone other than myself.

I accept that responsibility because I know there's something I could have done better as a coach to prepare my team. When you discover that you're your own worst critic, outside opinions and naysayers don't matter.

2. Improve Your Preparation: What can you do to achieve success the next time you're in a situation? The answer is simple: prepare. I don't believe in luck. Striking out at 9 to lose the city championship was the best thing that ever happened to me. When you feel pain like that, you'll do anything to avoid it again. It forced me to train and prepare harder.

I developed a mindset to either live with the pain of training and preparation or live with the pain of failure. I call it the fear of failure. I believe it's mankind's most powerful motivation. I began to use the strikeout as motivation. While training and practicing, I pushed myself to the point of exhaustion. I doubled the number of baseballs I hit, tripled the number of basketballs I shot and extended the amount of time I studied, because failure was no longer an option for me. I developed an intense work ethic. I've never considered myself the smartest, most talented or most gifted but no one is going to outwork me. It dates back to that day a 9-year-old struck out to lose the city championship.

3. Remember the moment: It took months for me to overcome the embarrassment of striking out. I felt humiliated, as if the world was watching my every move and laughing. Still after all these years, I fear I haven't completely purged that moment. Some days my mind drifts back to it. I'm standing there in disbelief.

Yet I have mourned the moment. While I've placed it in the category of ancient history, I'm still reminded. I went home that day and sought the comfort of my mother. She embraced me like only a mother could. I suffered through the teasing at The Boys & Girls Club. I tortured myself for months. The easy answer would have been to quit baseball and wallow in failure for the rest of my life. I wallowed in self-pity for six months and then slowly brushed off my shoulders to return. Time heals.

Within months, I felt awful about the mistake but not about myself. I started to separate the two. There was only so long I could torture myself. So I allowed myself to breathe. It was painful beyond measure. It was unpleasant and uncomfortable, but I had to find comfort in discomfort and take solace in the fact that there would be brighter days. As fate would have it, I found myself in the championship game once again the following year. I hit a three-run home run that allowed us to win our first city championship. I was named Most Outstanding Player.

Redemption.

CHAPTER 4

GUARDIAN ANGEL

"The two most important days of your life are the day that you are born and the day you figure out why."
Mattie McDougald

The phone rang a long time before I picked it up. My mother had decided to let it ring. It was April 1, 1984, April Fools' Day, and it was a rest day for my mom. Finally I answered it. It was my mother's best friend Faye, who asked to speak to my mother right away. I could hear the urgency in Faye's voice. I handed my mother the phone and stood in the kitchen listening, as nine-year-olds do.

"Oh my gosh," my mother said, dropping the phone. She began to pace.

"What's wrong?" I asked.

"Marvin Gaye died," she said.

"What?"

"He got shot," she said. "His daddy killed him."

Silence filled our kitchen. Marvin Gaye was a beloved musician.

The news was shocking. My mother instructed me to run and tell my grandmother. We lived on Jones Street, about a block away from her house on Lane Street. Running at top speed, I wondered, "Is this an April Fools' joke?" I burst into the backdoor that led to my grandmother's kitchen, met by the smell of home cooking and the warm face of Mattie Louise McDougald.

I could barely catch my breath. "What's wrong?" she asked.

"Marvin Gaye's dead," I shouted.

"What?"

"He got shot by his daddy," I said, trying to repeat what my mother had told me. My grandmother hugged me tight and rubbed my back for comfort. Dressed in her housecoat, she led me into the living room of her three-room house and turned on the small television set that was sitting on a large floor model. The story of Marvin Gaye's death was broadcast on every channel. The reports retold the R&B singer's life story and replayed his hit songs, such as "Let's Get It On" and "Sexual Healing." The reports described his death at the hands of his father the day before the singer's 45th birthday. This was tragic news in the black community, where Gaye was a giant star.

As the broadcast ended, a picture of Gaye flashed on the screen with his birth and death dates. My grandmother asked me to sit in her lap. She took out a pencil and wrote on a sheet of paper: April 2, 1939 – April 1, 1984. I sat quiet as a mouse.

"Do you see these dates?"

"Yes,"

She drew an X over everything but the dash. "As human beings we live and we die." The dates are beyond our control, she said. Ultimately the dates don't matter, she said, only the dash, because it's a person's legacy. She marked a dash clearly on the paper. "That's how people will remember you and how you will be judged."

Grandmothers are special souls. They see the world from a unique perspective. Their spirits are magnetic. Their voices are soothing yet powerful. Their words are encouraging and believable. And their love is infinite. When I was with my grandmother, I always felt like I was on top of the world. She swept me up in her tight embrace and handed down wisdom that I still follow. My top priority has been to make her proud of me.

My grandmother was born in 1920, when the country was segregated, didn't allow women to vote and blacks were forced to forgo an education and work as laborers in cotton and tobacco fields to earn a living. My grandmother never completed high school or attended college, but she never lacked intelligence. Her wisdom, passed down mostly in poetic sayings, serves as foundation for my life, my basketball program and my family.

My grandmother was a spiritual woman who believed in the power of prayer. She prayed multiple times throughout the day and her faith helped her raise six children. She carried her Bible at all times. When I was young and visited her house in Raleigh, she would make me get on my knees and pray beside her. Her prayers rang in my ears as eloquent haiku. As she prayed, I closed one eye, but spied on her with the other eye. She thanked God for everything.

She started each day with the Lord's Prayer, "Our father, which art in heaven, Hallowed be thy name. ..." Then she followed that with a serenity prayer. I don't really remember much else, but I noticed she would always end by asking God to bless not only her kids but her kid's kids. At six years old, I didn't know what that meant. I would later learn.

My grandmother's nickname for me was "Puffy" because I was a chubby baby. I don't think I ever heard her call me Velle. I was an inquisitive child and found excitement in sitting on the porch with her while she told stories about her hardships in life, limited opportunities for jobs and education and the racial injustice that

African Americans received during her era. Her stories about the civil rights movement were intriguing yet horrifying. I couldn't believe that blacks were lynched, denied voting rights, spat on, bitten by dogs and forced to sit in the back of the bus. She became my first history teacher.

I understand why she was such a spiritual lady: God was the only constant, dependable force she trusted. She introduced me to Martin Luther King Jr. His marches, beliefs and nonviolent demonstrations baffled me. "Granny, how could he not fight back, because I would hate someone who treated me that way." She leaned over and said in her soft voice, "Puffy, he's found peace in knowing that's what he was put on Earth to do."

That was a precious jewel I'd remember forever. But there were so many beneficial strands of advice. She said, "Puffy, I always want you to remember something. The two most important days of your life are the day that you are born and the day you figure out why."

Those who find peace and happiness find joy forever. My grandmother was such a humble spirit. She worked as a nurse and housekeeper (similar to the movie "The Help") for upper-class folks around Raleigh. She didn't make much money but she would give a stranger her last dollar if he or she needed it. There were bums and crack heads on the corner for whom she cooked a hot meal, and she would ask me to deliver it to them. She gave money to anyone who needed help to pay rent. Many people stopped by the house, and she prayed with them.

As a boy, I witnessed her kindness, forgiveness and unselfishness. There was a young guy, in particular, who was often in her living room, along with his significant other, studying the Bible with my granny. He was in divinity school at Shaw University. My grandmother taught him Bible verses and eventually helped him pastor his first church. When he began, he opened a modest church in a basement with about 20 members. His church grew exponentially. That young man was Pastor Frank Summerfield of Word of God Christian Church, which is one of the biggest churches in the Southeast. The church's school houses one of the most powerful basketball programs in the United States, nurturing such talents as C.J. Leslie, T.J. Warren and John Wall, the No. 1 overall selection in the 2011 NBA Draft. It's safe to say my granny's presence was monumental.

I had the most amazing granny on the planet. How could I be so fortunate? We became inseparable, and I soon found myself doing things for her approval. If I made up my bed, I asked, "Granny, are you proud of me?" If I took out the trash, I asked, "Granny, are you proud of me?" If I made an A on a test or scored 30 points, I asked, "Granny, are you proud of me?" Her approval mattered most and the more she said, "Yes, Puffy, I'm so proud of you," the more motivated I became to make her proud.

I attended church two to three times per week, traveled with her to the grocery store and just hung out on her porch enjoying the day. Eventually we became roommates. I moved from home up the street to live with my grandmother. After her long workdays, I prepared a hot bucket of water for her to soak her feet. I followed that with a foot massage until she fell asleep. I loved, worshipped and adored the ground she walked on.

One day my mother told my brother and me that she would be home a little late because she was taking my grandmother to the doctor for a checkup. I didn't think much of it. But then my mother soon told me I needed to move back home with her because my grandmother had to be hospitalized. This took me by surprise. She told me my grandmother was sick but would be home soon. My instincts, though, told me there was something more. I was not allowed to visit my granny in the hospital. My mother spent every night at the hospital, returning home in the morning to prepare me for school.

Family members visited town by the dozens. Some were strangers to me. One day through the thin walls of my bedroom I overheard my mother and her sister-in-law talking. "The doctors are going to have to remove one of her breasts because the cancer has spread," my mother said. I was 10 and didn't know anything about breast cancer. It might as well have been a cold or flu.

My granny was superwoman, the strongest person that I knew. I missed her and looked forward to her return home, where we could sit on the porch and talk. But it didn't work out that way. Days turned into weeks and weeks turned into months. Our only form of communication was a phone conversation once a day. Soon even these conversations decreased.

She eventually returned home and I moved back in with her for a while. Some days she didn't have strength, so I helped her around the house. I enjoyed bringing her butter pecan ice cream, her favorite. She loved when I rubbed cocoa butter on her feet. I felt like part of the healing process and was dedicated to her wellness. During that time, she introduced me to cherries, which I still can't resist today. I later learned the association between cherries and cancer, but at the time I had no idea how the disease had slowly deteriorated her vital organs.

March 1, 1986 is a day I will remember forever. Returning from the Boys & Girls Club to our apartment, I noticed the front door was slightly open. That was unusual. I thought someone had burglarized our home for a second time. I pushed the door open slowly and tiptoed in. The house was pitch-black and I began to hear sniffling from my mother's room. I made my way to her and cut the lights on. My mother was lying in the fetal position in the middle of the floor. She couldn't hide her pain, crying uncontrollably like a newborn.

My heart dropped to my stomach. I had never seen my mother cry, much less sob. I remained quiet. I sat on the floor and held her in my arms, wiping her tears and squeezing her as tight as I could. I grabbed her phone and started to dial – one by one I went through each name and number. I called to tell them that my grandma had died.

I knew the only thing in this world that could subject my mom to that kind of misery was the death of my grandmother.

What now? Once again, just like when my father left, I was at a crossroads. I struggled with fear of abandonment. The loss of my grandmother hurt, wounding me deeply and creating a scar that would never heal. I didn't see any reason to live because my driving force, my inspiration and my soul mate was no longer living. Still I had to remain strong for my mother. I worried about her health and state of mind. She had reached a dark state I had never witnessed. I felt helpless and hopeless. I was too young to take on the responsibility of keeping my family together. I felt like the little boy in the movie "Soul Food," who desperately tried to keep everyone together.

I don't remember many details about the funeral. However, I vividly remember standing over her casket and staring. In the streets, you're taught that men stand strong and firm. You're taught to never break down, cry or show emotions because crying is considered weakness. I was pushed to my limits at the burial site, but I held firm and dry-eyed. My entire family, especially my mother, lost control when they lowered my grandmother's body into the ground.

In the weeks that followed, a dysfunctional divide separated our family. You could only describe it as mayhem. My mother, uncles, aunts and other relatives began to argue over my grandmother's most prized possessions and valuables. Fights broke out. Arguments ensued. Things went from terrible to irreconcilable. The rock of our family was no longer there to mediate battles and settle arguments. Thus chaos. My mother, the youngest of six children and primary caretaker of my grandmother, became furious in response to her siblings' actions. My relatives distributed belongings among themselves, apparently in a manner that my grandmother hadn't assigned. In protest, my mother disconnected herself from her brothers and sisters.

This was no temporary departure. To this day, my mom has not spoken to my aunts or uncles in more than 25 years.

Family members grabbed what they perceived as valuable, taking jewelry, televisions and her radio. My mother was left with my grandmother's Bible and a few more items. She stored the Bible in a sacred place, and declared that that Bible "should never be touched." It was a Bible my granny carried everywhere. Inside, she had circled important scriptures and notes. She used that Bible to store important documents. I would find out in my adulthood just how important.

Twenty years later, when I closed on my first mortgage, my interior designer told me that a Bombay table would look great at the entrance of my home. However, we needed to add an ornament. I asked my mother if I could have my grandmother's Bible. She walked away and returned from her storage place and handed it to me.

With that Bible placed in my atrium, I forgave all of the foolishness my family went through 20 years before. I had my grandmother's most prized possession. That was priceless.

The Bible has remained at the entrance of my home for years. Before I begin every day, I place both hands on it and pray. It has become such a ritual that I can't leave the house with completing that task first. My daughter Brooke has reminded me several times when I've rushed out the door.

One day, the Bible was slightly off center. As I picked it up to center it, a piece of paper fell out. I unfolded the letter, noticed my grandmother's handwriting and began reading. What I read paralyzed me. I stood there overwhelmed by a prayer letter she had written to God before she died, asking him to watch over her family.

She wrote, "God, please bless my children and keep a loving hand on all of them especially Hattie [my mother], because you know she takes things to heart." The hairs on the back of my neck stood up. I could hear the vibrancy of her voice as I read every word of the letter. Tears rolled down my face.

The end of the letter sent me into a spasm. It read, "Father God, please bless my kid's kids. Put your loving arms around them and enlighten their minds, bodies and souls. Help them and protect them from their enemies. Grant them the serenity to accept the things they cannot change, courage to change the things that they can, and the wisdom to know the difference. Especially Puffy."

I called my mother, crying. She was silent on the phone yet I know she was crying. I had just moved into my home and all I asked her for was that Bible and she gave it to me. It was as if my grandmother had pulled out that letter and set it on the floor for me to read.

I told my mother, "After all these years, everyone thought they were taking valuables by grabbing her superficial items, but they were wrong." The most valuable item was her Bible. That's what my family needed.

INSIDE THE

LOCKER ROOM

The two most important days of your life are the day that you're born and the day you figure out why. Because of my granny, I've been able to figure out both. She helped me acknowledge my purpose on this earth, which is to use basketball as a metaphor to instill life skills and values in young people, and to help those less fortunate. Winning games and championships feels fantastic; however, nothing excites me more than giving back to others in need.

Granny once told me, "You can tell a lot about a person by the way they treat those that can do absolutely nothing for them." With my grandmother in mind, I launched the Velle Cares Foundation. Each year, we hold a back-to-school Community Day, a Father/Daughter Dance and a Single Mother's Salute, where the ultimate goal is to give back. Our mission is to assist community-based organizations that promote education, health and life skills for children and families at risk. None touched my heart more than a young lady by the name of Leah Ward.

Reading the paper one morning, I learned about an organization that was hosting a prom for people with terminal illnesses and those who had missed their proms because of illness. Having missed my prom, I called and volunteered to be someone's date. That's how I became connected with Leah Ward, who at 35 has been diagnosed with Williams Syndrome – a rare neurodevelopmental disorder that affects physical and mental development.

We have been friends since that prom night in 2011, when I pulled up to her house in a pink limousine. Leah's affable personality and witty charm put me at ease. We danced among others with terminal illnesses, and it was one of the most awe-inspiring events I've ever attended. They didn't feel sorry for themselves because of their troubles. Their spirits touched my heart, especially Leah's. Her smile swept me off my feet.

I've kept in touch with Leah, calling, texting and visiting. I've invited her to speak to my team in the locker room and watch games from the stands. I've learned more about her illness, but most important, I've learned more about her as a person. The night we met, I teased that she couldn't just take me out on a date and dump me. A dance brought us together but we remained friends because we need each other. I think my grandmother would agree.

The scariest part of my journey as a man is that I've had to figure life out myself. Manhood, fatherhood,

coaching and being a husband were things that frightened me initially because I never had an example to
show me how they are done. With time, I've advanced
in my life, professional career and as a person because
I'm the recipient of my grandmother's prayers from more
than 30 years ago. She knew in her heart that she would
not have an opportunity to see this day herself, so she
asked God to watch over me throughout my life journey.
I'm so glad He did. I try to live my life and respond to
life's situations the way she would. I still begin each day
by placing my hands on her Bible and asking God to
watch over my family.

I wake up with the sole intent of making my
grandmother proud. On March 15, 2014, our N.C.
Central basketball team faced Morgan State in a game
broadcast on ESPNU for the MEAC Championship. With
10 seconds remaining, it became evident we would
make history and capture the school's first conference
championship in 64 years. My senior guard, Alfonzo
Houston, approached the foul line and I could hear
my granny's voice. "Puffy, I'm so proud of you baby;
I'm so proud of you." My emotions slowly slipped from
my control. It seemed as though every hardship, pitfall
and setback from my life flashed before my eyes. My
guardian angel had protected me with her prayers and
devotion. The crowd in Norfolk Scope Arena erupted

with a loud roar, and I glanced at the Jumbotron above my head and saw myself. The crowd had reacted to my tears flashed on the screen. Later at the press conference, I answered questions about the moment, though I couldn't stop thinking about my granny.

When anyone asks me why or how, I tell a story about my granny, a praying woman who asked God to watch over me. Her Bible will always be on the Bombay table when you enter my home. On top of that Bible is a program from her funeral printed with a eulogy. On the front it reads, "Mattie Louise McDougald, December 10, 1920 – March 1, 1986." But as she taught me, it's not the birth or death years that matter, it's the dash, because that's how she will be remembered.

CHALKBOARD

1. Overcome Adversity: "Adversity introduces a man to himself." It's a quote that's served as my mantra. Adversity happens at a specific time and forces us to look in the mirror and deal with the harsh reality of ourselves, as well as our present circumstances. It's a fact of life. None of us is immune to adversity, but you fight and persevere. Adversity can't be controlled or measured, but the only control we have is how we respond to the situation. I've seen so many people who were gifted and talented but not tough enough to respond to adversity, so they gave up hope. Life isn't fair, and it surely doesn't care about your feelings, so be prepared.

2. Find your Purpose: Place your hand over your heart. Do you feel that? Do you feel your heart beating? That's called purpose. Finding your purpose on this earth is the greatest accomplishment for any individual. However, understand that there's a difference between what you've been put here to do and what you think you've been put here to do. Therefore be honest with yourself.

I had NBA dreams. In 1996, I was named CIAA Player of the Year over Ben Wallace, who later became the NBA Defensive Player of the Year. He earned more than $60 million, and I went overseas to play professionally. After four seasons, I began a teaching career. I had to accept the fact that the NBA was not my calling. Life has granted me perspective and clarity because I know I've been put on this earth to serve and assist those who are less fortunate. I'm happy with my role.

3. Power of Prayer: My grandmother's death remains an unhealed wound. But I've accepted that "The Lord giveth, but He taketh away." Life is brutal and often times you will find yourself wondering why it is treating you so unkind. The daily temptations of this world will take the soul of a man and turn him upside down. At an early age, I was taught the power of prayer, the act of simply getting on my knees and asking God for what I require. I ask God for knowledge, healing, serenity and protection of my family. Those are things I've made a part of my daily regimen. The power of prayer works. Living in the projects and escaping unscathed with knowledge and wisdom is a credit to God – not me.

CHAPTER 5

HOT SHOT

*"A person often meets his destiny on
the road he took to avoid it."*
Jean de la Fontaine, French poet

There are good days so unexpected you wonder what God was thinking when ordering your life. In 1985, when I was 11, I walked to the Raleigh Boys & Girls Club after school, cutting through neighborhoods and projects between the club and our apartment. I spent almost every day at the club, summertime included. They called me a "club kid." Raleigh Boys & Girls director Ralph Capps told me, "If you weren't there, we would say, 'I wonder where LeVelle is today?'" I knew about most activities – field trips to museums, holiday parties – and participated in every sport offered, especially baseball and basketball.

It took about 20 minutes to walk to the club from my house on Jones Street, even though I knew shortcuts and walked pretty fast through the neighborhoods. One day I reached the parking lot and spotted a huge, white Pepsi truck that looked like a delivery vehicle. Perhaps they were restocking the snack machines, I thought. Curious as always, I rushed into the club to see what was happening. I was told the club was hosting the Pepsi Hot Shot Challenge.

My friends explained that it was a basketball-shooting contest and encouraged me to enter. They were pumped about my chances of winning. I declined, not really interested in the game. Then I saw a long table topped with two-liter Pepsi bottles. Someone said the winner got two free bottles of soda. Okay, that changed my mind. I could drink a two-liter Pepsi without stopping – seriously, I wasn't bothered by the fizzle or the throat burn. I'd drop my head back and guzzle soda like water.

Ron Williams, the director of programs, signed me up. Ron started as my mentor and became my godfather. He looked out for me and taught me so many things about young adulthood and growing into a young man. He explained the rules of the Pepsi challenge after my friends unsuccessfully tried. The idea was to shoot from the round rubber mats on the floor. Contestants got 60 seconds. "Just shoot the ball as many times as you can from as many spots as you can and make them," Ron said. Simple.

As everyone prepared for the contest, there was a song that played, "Hot shot, show us what you got." I couldn't erase the tune from my mind for months. As I watched, what I needed to do became clear. It was advantageous to get to every spot twice, because you collected bonus points. The time started when the music did.

I hadn't come to the club to participate in a shooting competition, but I was always ready to shoot. I had built a solid reputation as a shooter and that's why my friends were so anxious for me to play. When I was younger, Ron kept moving me to higher levels. The basketball goal started at eight feet, then moved to nine feet, and then jumped to 10 feet. So when I was eight, I played with the big kids on a 10-foot basket. I was short, weak and skinny, so I'd take a shot from low and double-clutch it to lift it up there consistently. That became my right-handed shot – a herky-jerky hitch shot. Even now my shot has a little jerk, a little awkwardness. Some called it ugly. I thought it was pretty. But shooting at the higher goal is how I developed better form and longer range.

Both came in handy as I joined the Hot Shot competition. All eyes were on me as I started quickly, draining shots. With every shot I made, people hollered my name, which was simultaneously exhilarating and scary. I remembered Ron's advice, "Don't stop until time stops." My hand caught fire and I couldn't miss. After I was done, kids rushed the floor, congratulating me and celebrating. I didn't quite know why until the organizer announced I had broken a record.

"What record?"

"The local points record."

"How much did I score?

"63."

I won the local competition and was entered in the state competition. "You get to go to Charlotte and shoot against everyone else who won the local competition," the organizer said.

"Thank you," I said, collecting my certificate and my two bottles of Pepsi. Don't underestimate how important those sodas were to me.

With time to practice, the Hot Shot half-court setup played naturally to my strengths. There was a mat at the top of the key, two mats in the three-point corners, and one mat on each low block line. You had to make contact with the mats, so I practiced touching them with my feet but leaning forward to shoot. That propelled me faster across the court to chase the ball down, miss or make. I figured out, while I was shooting from one side, how to race to the other side to shoot. I was about 90 percent right most of the time. I didn't take bonus shots from the corners because it took too long to hunt the ball down. "I didn't have to tell you, 'LeVelle, you need to practice for your Pepsi Hot Shot.' You came in and started practicing," Ron recalled. I loved basketball, so it was no chore to take shots. I mastered the strategy and my technique quickly paid dividends.

I kept cool in Charlotte. I sized up the competition and felt confident about my chances. These kids were serious. Many of them, dressed in uniforms and Pepsi apparel, appeared as if they had trained an entire summer for that moment. They warmed up with fancy routines and swished shots. Their parents were armed with video cameras and signs. My mother was at work. I still was not sure if the Hot Shot Challenge was where I wanted to spend my free time. I felt bad for beating those guys. I didn't feel as much pressure as they did and was relaxed when I performed.

"State competition just didn't faze you," Ron said. "That was the amazing thing."

I easily won the competition in Charlotte, advancing to the Atlanta regional round.

I decided to have fun in Atlanta. Why not? It was a road trip with my man Ron, who presented himself like a curt, cranky, curmudgeonly old football coach. He was hilarious. You couldn't help laughing at how serious he was. His idea of affirmation was saying, "Next in line." He was hardcore old school. He demanded respect, yet he gave it back. He cared about us. So it was Ron, me and Terry Niles, who qualified for the regional event in another age group. We rode down in a rented van. Ron had already chided and comforted me before we left Raleigh, explaining, "LeVelle, if you practice, you know, you could win it." Sure, whatever.

But I listened and started practicing after school, taking shots from everywhere. I loved shooting the rock. There were many nights I shot past eight o'clock at the Boys & Girls Club, and Ron drove me home.

Ron continued his lecture on the way to Atlanta. "The thing you've got to do is have confidence in yourself," he said. "You understand what I'm saying?"

"Yes."

"You know you've got to focus."

"Yes."

My only knowledge of Atlanta, really, was that Martin Luther King Jr. had lived there and that a madman, Wayne Williams, had been accused of murdering black children on a killing spree there. I was young when that happened, but I remember it bothering my mother. She wanted me in the house all the time. From 1979-81, a rash of child murders disrupted Atlanta life and made headlines around the country. That scared me and made me cautious.

However, we felt safe with Ron, a former N.C. Central University football player who didn't take mess from anyone. He was short, but everyone thought he was Superman because of his chiseled muscles. Besides, we were there to find out what was so special about the Pepsi regional event.

We arrived in Atlanta and checked into our hotel, some ways from a huge recreation center in Decatur where the event was being held. There were so many kids it looked like a graduation ceremony. Everyone had to register at 9 a.m., and it seemed to take forever. There were several courts throughout the gym, each marked with rubber mats to indicate shooting positions. No surprises there.

Ron continued to feed us positive messages, "You got to be confident."

"I am."

"You know these are the things I expect to see out of you?"

"Yes."

"You know these are the things that you've got to do to be successful."

"Okay."

My mind wandered a little from Ron as I watched the other kids shoot. In line, there were whispers about who was the one to beat. There were several opinions about one kid dressed in everything Pepsi, apparently sponsored by the company. He had on Pepsi socks. He had a Pepsi headband. We joked he had on Pepsi drawers. This is where people play head games, faking you out with how they are dressed, as if clothes have anything to do with how well they can shoot. I thought, *This kid must be nice.* Luckily, Ron had drilled in our minds to focus.

Each participant in each age group competed in three rounds. Waiting through so many contestants wracked my nerves. I've never liked sitting on the bench while others played.

The Pepsi Kid scored 50 in his opening round. I followed with 50 points. We traded buckets in the second round like Bird and Magic. That set the stage for a winner-take-all third round. Word quickly spread around the gym. The Pepsi Kid, having won several years in row, was the crowd favorite. I was my momma's favorite but she wasn't there.

It was the Pepsi Kid vs. Lane Street. To start the final round, The Pepsi Kid shot first. He scored 57 points, the highest total of the round. Excited and confident of a win, he held his follow-through for what seemed like 10 minutes after his last shot, saying, essentially, "I got this." I gave him credit. He showed out. He was nice.

I needed 60 points to win. No problem.

Using a soft shooter's touch and rhythm, I dropped 63, and the crowd erupted in cheers. People rushed over and picked me up. The announcer said I had earned a spot in the finals and would shoot before a national television audience during halftime at a Washington Bullets and Chicago Bulls game.

"Damn," I said, collecting the award, momentarily excited by the thought of shooting at a NBA game.

Days later, after the euphoria passed, my feelings changed. Back in Raleigh, comfortable in my routine, I started to dread the next phase of the Hot Shot. I was bored with it.

I had entered the Pepsi Hot Shot Challenge to satisfy my selfish thirst. Two bottles of the good stuff and I was done. I wasn't interested in being the best 12-year-old shooter in the country. That sounded corny. It sounded soft. Real basketball players played real games. I put my heart and soul into Amateur Athletic Union basketball games. You could be the best Hot Shot competitor in the world and still not get any run on my home court or at the Boys & Girls Club. I might be a champion shooter but no one would respect me as a basketball player, I thought. I wanted to avoid that. I couldn't live with that.

Plus, I'd need to travel to Washington, D.C., to shoot at halftime of a NBA game on the same day I was supposed to play AAU basketball. That sounded lame. I didn't want to miss a game to go shoot somewhere. How do you explain that to your boys?

Weeks passed and the organization mailed letters to my mother. I opened the mail, and the organization had sent itineraries and plane tickets. I was hiding all of this information in my room, hoping my mother wouldn't discover it. I wasn't going. One night, I hear my mother on the phone. "Oh, he's going," she said. Apparently, the organization had called the Raleigh Boys & Girls Club to find out my status, and Ron called my mother. I made my case, informing them both of my very important AAU tournament. Ron explained to my mother that my representing the club was a huge deal. There were only three kids left in the nation, he told her, and I was one of them. He told her about the educational opportunities to see the monuments and the sites. I started crying, hoping my tears would have some effect, but knowing I had about a two percent chance of convincing my mother. "Don't worry, his butt is going," she told Ron.

That was that. I boarded a plane for the first time, heading to Washington, D.C. I didn't think much of the experience until we reached National Airport and through the window the monuments filled the sky. As a kid from the hood, I rarely left my four-block radius of projects and mayhem. Now I was flying into town on some legit business. And quietly, I'm a history buff. I was seeing things I had only read about in school.

Ron and I toured the city, stopping by the Jefferson Memorial and the Lincoln Memorial, where Dr. Martin Luther King Jr. made his speech. Finally, we visited the White House, and I was surprised and confounded: There were homeless people camped around the gates. Who would believe homeless people lived near the White House? It reminded me of my neighborhood because of the proximity of the Lane Street projects to the Governor's Mansion. I could ride my bike three blocks and deliver the paper to the governor. In fact, my friends and I would circle the mansion, trying to see inside. I wondered how Gov. James G. Martin, a Republican, could live so well and the rest of the people down the street live so poorly. No one had an answer for me. And then I go to Washington, D.C., and see the same thing at the White House, of all places. *Don't you see these people need help?* Something wasn't right.

I had been wrong in complaining about the trip. I experienced moments that changed my life. I saw there was a life outside of the projects for me. I remember praying to God: "Thank you for letting me see this." God had allowed me to witness the highest levels of human suffering, giving me something to overcome, and then shown me a vision of something better. I had no desire to be president, but I never wanted to be a homeless person sleeping in front of the White House. I wanted to help whoever had fallen into that predicament.

I felt nervous throughout the competition but nothing like when I walked into the Capital Centre in Landover, Md., where the Washington Bullets (now Washington Wizards) held home games. Sections in the arena seemed higher than the monuments we had toured. The court felt extra large. The hoops seemed higher. The floor shone brighter. There were television cameras at both ends of the court.

All this reminded me that the competition would be viewed live. I started worrying. My friends and family were looking at this game at home. Cramps grabbed my insides and squeezed. I felt dizzy and lightheaded. I needed water. Man, I was scared.

Then as we were walking onto the floor for the competition, the Chicago Bulls came off the court, heading to the locker room for halftime. I was sure I had fallen into a dream world because we rarely saw professional players where I was from. Michael Jordan, who I had followed religiously at North Carolina, walked by me and rubbed my head, saying, "All right, little fellow." OMG. I lost it. I never recovered.

Michael Jordan - raised in North Carolina and a legend in my state while in high school - had touched my head. I had written poems about Michael Jordan. I had watched him dash Georgetown's dreams in the NCAA Tournament. I knew all of his stats. This was his first season in the NBA. Who would believe I met him? It was crazy.

I don't remember much about the competition except that I came in second. With my stomach in knots and head on cloud nine, it didn't matter. I respected the winner.

"I think you were nervous at first," Ron said. "But once you got out on the floor, it just became natural. Because you can shoot."

His words made me feel good.

Ron said one of my shots fell short and rolled loose during the two-round competition. That cost me.

Still, the final score was close. I had experienced a lot in a short time by competing in the challenge. It was all unexpected, but I delighted in the experience like it was my birthday.

INSIDE THE

LOCKER ROOM

I came home from Washington, D.C. a different person. And to think, I hadn't even wanted to go. I learned it was perfectly fine to try new things. I stepped out into the world and discovered a fascinating new place. Even more important, I made a connection between where I lived and the seat of our government. No one was immune to problems, and we all had to play our part to solve them.

After the kid beat me on national TV, I gained new respect for the competition. The Pepsi Kid had been a great shooter. It took everything I had to compete against him. Every new level presented a stiffer challenge.

That's how life has worked out. If you don't come prepared to work and execute, you will be sent home with a tear in your eye. You can't win everything but you can prepare for everything. Preparation, arriving knowing you practiced until it hurt, allows you to walk without feelings of regret.

I realized you have to compete with all your heart to be great, and I set that as my new standard. Every time I stepped on the court, I wanted to shoot at an elevated level. I wasn't wasting time anymore. I wanted to destroy my opponent. My work ethic changed from mediocre to acceptable, and then I learned how to raise it to another level: remarkable. Competing so well boosted my confidence, which allowed me to make personal changes.

People noticed something different about me. "You walked differently," Ron told me years later. I saw where my potential could take me if I stayed on a positive course. The lesson was relatable to basketball and school. I understood what my teachers, coaches and everyone else who was trying to redirect my behavior was saying. I understood that lazy attempts at greatness were useless. The more I applied myself, the more support I received. People started rooting for me. It was the first time my abilities had taken me outside of the projects. It foreshadowed what I could achieve if I worked hard.

As others rooted for me, I discovered my true desire to play basketball.

Participating in the Pepsi Hot Shot Challenge, I realized how much I loved shooting. I recognized my athletic strength, which was bolstered by mental strength. I could concentrate on a subject for a long time and complete a task. Coach could put me in the game and tell me to score and I would try every tactical way to score. My shot was better than most, but I used my skills to get the job done. My mind rarely wandered off-task. This self-recognition of my talents convinced me that basketball might be my best sport, even though I could knock the cover off a baseball and throw a football 50 yards. You have to examine your skill set and make serious choices about who you are athletically and academically.

As long as I played basketball, shooting accurately factored into my repertoire. I led my middle school, high school and college in scoring. I averaged 30 points per game in high school and scored a school-record 51 points. I became the third all-time leading scorer for my university, producing 1,714 points during my four-year career.

More than anything, I learned to get out of my own way. I almost allowed my desire to do what I knew keep me from experiencing a plane ride for the first time. That's ironic, considering I'm always boarding a plane these days. I almost missed the experience of touring Washington, D.C., where I discovered something about myself: I'm an advocate for the underdog. Seeing those people homeless in front of the White House remained in my mind. As part of my life's mission, I help those in need through giving. That's the wonderful legacy of a competition I didn't want to enter.

CHALKBOARD

1. Compete: As iron sharpens iron, so one man sharpens another. I've always been in competition. I compete in basketball, golf, coloring with my daughter, and since I was a kid, with my older brother. I admired him and wanted to grow up just like him. If he played a sport, I had to play that sport. But I wanted to be better than him. It's the nature of brothers, loving each other yet fiercely battling for supremacy. Verne was five years older, so we really weren't in the same group. Still I challenged him, building a natural competitive streak, a character trait I carry to this day. I never backed down because my brother was older and stronger. Sibling rivalry prepared me for competition at all levels.
I'm thankful for my brother because he served as a nemesis for years. Many times he didn't even know we were competing. I measured my success by how well I did compared to him.

It's important to seek out competition. Place yourself in difficult scenarios and study how you respond. Compete with peers. Compete with strangers. Sports provide a testing ground but there are other activities. Compete in school. If your best friend receives a high score, challenge yourself to earn a better score next time. If your co-worker completes tasks faster, challenge yourself to pick up the pace. It's healthy. It's necessary. It's essential for growth.

Every great individual had a rival who brought out the best in him or her. Steve Jobs had Bill Gates, Coke has Pepsi, LeBron has Kobe. Ultimately we are judged by wins and losses. The more competitive you are, the greater chance you have of winning.

2. Become Well-Rounded: I meet many kids who are one-dimensional. They focus on one specific craft and hinder themselves. They don't realize that one skill assists others. Since I enrolled at the Boys & Girls Club, I've enjoyed trying different activities – arts and crafts, hiking, biking, fishing, golfing, tennis. I didn't like everything, but I'd usually participate. I'm glad I tried the Pepsi Hot Shot Challenge on a lark. The experience showed me the value of trying different things. Something unfamiliar turned into a special journey. Whenever I get stuck doing things the same way, I'm reminded of the Hot Shot Challenge, and I know it's time to try something different. I'm usually rewarded for my bravery.

It's difficult to try new things. Humans find their comfort zones and scoff at change. When you reach that stubborn place, challenge yourself and reward yourself for trying something different. Being open-minded about something that initially doesn't seem appealing is a must. It removes you from your comfort zone and allows you to become a student all over again.

3. Mama Knows Best: I believe in the power of mother's intuition. My mother has never been the type to intervene when it came to me playing sports. However, I am so grateful she insisted that I go to Washington, D.C., and represent the Boys & Girls Club. At the time I rebelled. I was seeing the world through the eyes of a stubborn 11-year-old who had convinced himself there was no "street credibility" in a shooting competition. Boy was I wrong.

The failed attempt to hide plane tickets was just one blessing in disguise. My mother didn't know a thing about basketball, but she knew this was a chance of a lifetime for her baby boy, a chance to see beyond my circumstances.

Boarding a plane for the first time was thrilling. I remember watching the monuments against the blue sky above Washington, D.C. The real life statues replaced pictures from books. The experience enriched my life. Once I returned, I looked forward to the next destination. If you come to a crossroads with your parents, take my advice and listen to them.

I'm sure glad I did because Mama knows best.

FROM COACH MOTON'S PHOTO ALBUM

Mom, Verne and me during Christmas in 1980.

My brother Verne
and I.

My old apartment
in Raleigh, N.C.

Playing with my HERO; my mother Hattie McDougald.

At home with my grandmother, Mattie McDougald.

Major League Dreams

Hot Shot Days

On the move at Enloe High School.

Graduation Day at N.C. Central in 1996.

"Poetry 'N Moton"

My mother, Hattie McDougald, and me.

My wife, Bridget, and daughter, Brooke, and me.

My "Guardian Angel" watching over me moments before N.C. Central wins the MEAC Championship.

Intense coaching during the 2013–14 NCAA Tournament.

Words of Inspiration   **My first ever college game coaching in 2009–10.**

Photos courtesy of North Carolina Central University

**Embracing my seniors, Jeremy Ingram and Alfonzo Houston, during the
2013–14 NCAA Tournament.**

Celebrating with seniors Emanuel Chapman and Jeremy Ingram after
capturing MEAC Tournament.

A handful – my
son, Velle Jr.,
and daughter,
Brooke.

Photo courtesy of North Carolina Central University

Cutting down the
nets with Velle,
Jr., after winning
MEAC.

Family vacation
at Sea World and
Disney World.

Brooke and I holding
The Rock.

Left: Holding VJ at UNC Burn Center during his recovery.

Right: Laughing with my mentor and godfather, Ron Williams, who worked at the Raleigh Boys & Girls Club.

Brooke in my arms during an interview after our victory at N.C. State during the 2013–14 season.

Photo courtesy of North Carolina Central University

Standing in line to receive my graduate degree in December 2013 at N.C. Central University.

Photo courtesy of North Carolina Central University

Above: My
Brothers,
My Inspirations,
New Edition.

MOTON STRONG

Luke 12:48 –
To whom much
is given, much is
required.

Champions.

N.C. Central University's 2013–14 men's MEAC Championship Team.

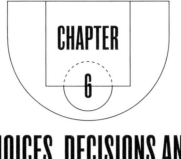

CHAPTER 6

CHOICES, DECISIONS AND CONSEQUENCES

*"It's better to walk alone than with a crowd
that's going in the wrong direction."*
Diane Grant

remember the cell door closing behind me. I turned and looked at my brother as if to say, "How in the world did we end up in here?" That's the moment I changed my life. I was done making bad choices. From then on, I would pick my friends much more carefully.

The Wake County jail smelled of old men and urine. I wanted to be in that small cell like you'd want to be in a burning building. I had learned my lesson. I got the point. No more foolishness. It was time for Sheriff John Baker Jr. to pop the lock and set me free.

"When did my mother say she'd be back?" I asked.

"Be back?" he asked, chuckling.

"Yeah," I said. "Seriously."

"Hour, two," he said.

That was one hour too long in that place. It hadn't taken me long to assess my surroundings: nasty. I wasn't built for jail life. I wasn't far from my 14th birthday and here I was locked down inside a facility with grown men who looked as if they belonged here, a long list of crimes explaining their pasts and futures. They were big and burly, ugly and surly and appeared to have nothing better to do than make my life a living hell. They were intimidating, staring through the steel bars with malicious intent. They cursed freely. They were an unhappy lot, incarcerated and dumped into the legal system. Their faces growled and scowled, even without making a sound. They hung on the bars, smoking cigarettes and wiping sweat from their furrowed brows.

My shirt was soaked, as if I were in a steam bath. But that would have been enjoyable. Standing in that cell was torture. The heat irritated me. I really didn't need a tour of this facility. I wasn't planning on coming back. I was rehabilitated. Scared straight.

"You'll be back," Baker said, "if you keep on messing around, doing what you're doing."

Tell the Truth

He was right. A week earlier, I had been sitting in a police station in downtown Raleigh answering questions about a murder.

Detective: Where were you around 5 o'clock today?

Me: At home.

Detective: What were you doing?

Me: Watching TV.

Detective: Do you know Blue and Sam from the Southside?

Me: Yes, they are my friends from around the neighborhood.

Detective: Where do you live?

Me: Jones Street.

Detective: You hang out much with Blue and Sam?

Me: Yeah, we see each other all the time. We ride bikes and shoot ball at the same court.

Detective: Did you go with them today to the convenience store?

Me: No.

Detective: When is the last time you saw them?

Me: Earlier today. We rode our bikes to the playground. We played basketball together. But I left them and went home around 3:30 because I wanted to watch my shows.

Detective: What shows?

Me: Every day I watch "Diff'rent Strokes" at 4, "What's Happening?" at 4:30, "Good Times" at 5 and "Sanford and Son" at 5:30. Then at 6 the news comes on and my mother watches the TV.

Detective: So you weren't riding your bike at the convenience store today?

Me: No.

Detective: Do you know anything about your friends robbing the convenience store? Was it planned? Did they plan to murder the clerk?

Me: I don't know anything about murder. No one said anything to me about robbing a store. I just went home.

Hard Times

A week before that Thursday, my life had been spiraling out of control. Call it teenage rebellion. I was angry and suddenly prone to making stupid decisions. I couldn't talk with my mother or brother, and my confidant, my grandmother, had died four years earlier from breast cancer. That had really rocked my world.

My grandmother was my heart. She lived in a shotgun house across from the basketball courts on Lane Street, four short blocks from our house on Jones Street. As far as grandmothers go, she fit the mold of a sweet, God-fearing woman who said her prayers morning and night, went to church on Sunday mornings and fed the hungry out of her house. If you needed something, you called on Mattie Louise McDougald.

What I needed was attention, and she created a platform for me to share my dreams. We talked. We kicked it. She had so much knowledge. And she was so spiritual. She introduced me to God. If today there were a fire at my house, I'd grab my children and my grandmother's worn black Bible. She used to read from it to me and quote scriptures. My mother didn't raise me in the church, but my grandmother made sure I had an elementary understanding of religion before she passed.

My grandmother listened to me. One day I told her that kids in my middle school class laughed at me because I wanted to be J.J. Evans from "Good Times" when I grew up. She told me, "Don't let anybody tell you what you're going to be when you grow up."

A month later, my grandmother invited me to church, supposedly to watch a Christmas play. When I arrived she handed me a robe and a towel and instructed me to put them on. She had landed me a part in the play as Joseph.

"Who is Joseph?"

"He's Jesus' father," she said. "Don't worry, I'll tell you what to say."

Years later I figured out why she wanted me to play Joseph in the Christmas play. My grandmother had placed me in the position to make my dreams come true. She didn't care if no one in my class believed I could grow to be an actor like "J.J. Evans." She believed. She handed me over to God and asked that He help me become who I wanted to be. I was too young and inexperienced to comprehend her plan at the time.

She was sick for a long time before she died on March 1, 1986. The only thing I remember about her funeral is standing over her casket and staring. I didn't think men were supposed to cry, so I held back my tears. I suppressed all of my emotions. I thought my family had lied to me about her illness. They told me she had had her breast removed, but I didn't connect her sickness with cancer.

Her death caused me more pain than I knew. In a short time, I had lost my father and my grandmother. I was just 10. It felt like every person I loved left me. *What was wrong with me? Did I drive them away?* They were silly thoughts but they felt real. I couldn't handle the outcome and started to misbehave. Over the next four years, I slowly turned into a juvenile delinquent.

I started fighting. If you said something to me out of the way, I would fight you. Put your hands up. My mother was at school every other week for a teacher conference or meeting. I was an intelligent student, but my behavior had started to affect my grades. My issues were spilling out around me, though no one recognized what was going on. Even at the Boys & Girls Club, I was threatening to fight grown-ups. There was a long stretch when I carried an attitude into every situation outside of my house. I say outside because my mother didn't allow backtalk and smart-aleck remarks in her home. She ran a tight ship and believed in discipline. If I forgot my place, she would whip me until I remembered. She was a tough lady. I didn't try her much, just avoided letting her see my silly antics.

My mother worked so much we hardly saw her. She worked as a domestic at the Velvet Cloak. Cleaning hotel rooms is back-breaking work. She stood for 14 hours, changing sheets, cleaning toilets, dumping trash, straightening furniture and vacuuming hallways. She came into the house with brooms and mops, half-dead, unable to keep her eyes open for "The Tonight Show With Johnny Carson." Her ankles would swell and I'd bring her a bucket to soak her feet in. Then I'd rub cheap shea cocoa butter on them. When she got home, she hardly made it past the couch. When she hit the bed, she slept like a corpse until she left for her part-time cleaning job. Working like a machine, she provided our family's only income and made her wages honestly.

After the bills were paid, there were few dollars left for recreational activities, what some people call "disposable income."

Sometimes she would offer me a food stamp. I could take that to the store and buy a 15-cent candy and have change for the rest of the day. Do the math and that's 85 cents for 12 hours when I went to the Boys & Girls Club. Guess how far that went?

To make money, I hustled games of H.O.R.S.E. and one-on-one basketball. But that yield was limited. Young kids had little money to gamble. So soon I was stealing lunches from other kids. I was stealing from the Winn-Dixie grocery store. My friends would go to the mall to steal, and I was right there with them. The things we stole amounted to little in cash but they were enough to change our meager situations for a day or two. I knew stealing was wrong. I wasn't raised that way. I didn't need to steal to survive.

One day, our luck changed when we were caught stealing stone-washed jeans from North Hills Mall. The cop took us downtown. He immediately recognized me and asked, "Do you want to go to jail, or do you want me to call your mother?" I replied, "Take me to jail." I wasn't a tough guy, and there was no way I wanted to de-liver that embarrassing news to my mother. I agreed to 20 cleanup hours at North Hills Mall. Thank God, my mother never knew or she would have killed me. As hard as she was working for my fu-ture, pushing brooms and scrubbing floors, she might have lost her mind.

It was the late 1980s and crack had gripped our community hard, just as it had landed in other U.S. cities. Drugs flooded the streets, and older hustlers and dealers wielding pockets full of money lured us into the dope game. These older dealers were targeted by the po-lice and would have received long sentences in the penitentiary un-der laws established by President Ronald Reagan's administration – the crack vs. powder cocaine debate. There was a so-called war on drugs, and dealers thought they were smart to recruit young kids to handle their drugs. The theory was that kids were not charged as adults and would receive lighter sentences for drug crimes.

My family's economic situation made it difficult to say no to fast money. My mother hated that I was hanging out daily at the mini-park. It was a place to perfect my game on the courts but also a place where you could easily find drugs, violence and prostitution. The older hustlers would sometimes ask us to take a brown paper bag to someone across the street. They played on our upbringings. When your elders asked you to do something, you did it. That's how we were trained. I would do it without really knowing what I was doing and receive $10 for my errand. After a few times walking across the street, I realized I wasn't delivering cookies and I quit. Thankfully, I never delved into hardcore drug selling. I didn't have the heart or stomach for drugs. I watched crack ruin people's lives. I knew drugs were poison.

Knock, Knock

Even though I wasn't handcuffed, walking into the police station made me feel like a criminal. I was there to be questioned like one. The police had come looking for me as if I were on the lam.

The knock on the door was surreal. We lived in a two-bedroom apartment on the bottom floor of a three-story building. Our living room was closest to the front door, with the kitchen off to the side. Two small bedrooms were in back.

My mother was in the kitchen starting dinner. I was in the living room. "Sanford and Son" had just ended and my mother had turned the television to the news. Leading the reports was a story about a murder at a convenience store.

There was a heavy knock on the door. *Bam! Bam! Bam!* A police knock is different from all other knocks. I don't know if they learn that in the academy but I recognized it right away. My mother told me to answer the door.

I opened the door and two police were standing there in uniform, radios abuzz. My eyes found their guns and then rolled back to their faces. They introduced themselves.

Police officer No. 1: Are you LeVelle Moton?

Me: Yes.

Police officer No. 2: Are your parents home?

Me: Yes.

Hearing the two voices, my mother peeked from inside the kitchen and said, "Come in."

The police informed her of what they knew and said they needed to ask me some questions down at the station. Someone had been killed. There had been a robbery. Kids were involved.

"That's his friends," my mother said.

My mother looked at me as if to say, "This is serious." She asked the police officers if she could drive me to the station. We drove downtown in silence. I kept thinking about how I could prove my innocence. My mother knew me as a good kid, but I had told a lie or two in my time. This was a different situation. This was murder. Did I need to convince her I wasn't a murderer? I hadn't been there. I had been at home. That's what I told detectives at the station.

Detective: Where did you go today?

Me: I left the house in the afternoon. I went to my friend's house. Then we hung outside. Then we all went to the basketball court on Lane Street.

Eventually the police released me. They had the other guys in custody, and they had told the police I wasn't with them at the convenience store. I loved my friends, but I loved "Good Times" more. Any other time, I would have been right there with them. That was scary.

They had robbed a store and committed murder. I couldn't believe it. These guys were my friends. My boys. They had bypassed the store we normally went to for candy, and rode their bikes farther away from the neighborhood. We occasionally rode our bikes to that store – it was about five blocks over – but that wasn't our first or second choice.

My friends went to the store looking for microwave sandwiches, which had just been introduced. Take one out of the big store freezer, put it in the microwave for 50 seconds and you had a hot sandwich or burrito. My friends didn't enter the store looking to make the evening news. They were hungry, hunting food and intending to steal. They arrived on BMX bikes and parked them outside.

While warming up the sandwiches, the plan took a turn for the worse. The clerk came from behind the counter and approached them. They were surprised. Every time I think of the scene, I'm reminded of the movie "Juice," where the main character, Bishop, who is carrying a gun, overreacts while his crew is robbing a small neighborhood convenience store. With the click of a pistol, the situation went in a new, terrible direction. The clerk was killed.

My friends were arrested, charged, tried and convicted. They were just kids. Yet they served time at a reformatory facility and then in a correctional facility as adults. I think about that day all the time. We never discussed robbing the store, so I can't say I chose to not commit a crime with them. I chose to watch TV.

Scared To Death

My mother chose to teach me a lesson.

"This is not the way to go," she told me. "You have to pick better friends."

"I didn't know they were going to shoot anyone," I said, which was kind of a true-false statement. I didn't know my friends were going to rob that store and one of them would end up killing someone. But I knew they carried guns because several people in my crew carried guns. I don't want to misrepresent who we were. We weren't tough kids who bullied others and ran around like a gang, destroying things. We were not gangbangers or cowboys. For the most part, we were peaceful kids who rode our bikes. As the neighborhood turned, with drugs ruining lives and guns easier to find, some members of our crew gravitated to more danger-ous behavior.

We didn't really need pistols, yet they made life manageable. Our neighborhood had become like the wild, wild West, and those on the frontier needed to know we had the latest in technology, such as bullets and handguns. Protect yourself: That was the code.

It went like this: *These bad dudes over there need to know that I have this gun, even though inside I'm petrified of what it can do and I'm like, "Please don't ever make me use this."* That's a complicated psychology, but I was raised in an urban jungle where the rules were different from other environments' rules. I followed those rules until I found myself in a Wake County jail cell, looking at real criminals who lived by an even more complicated psychology than mine.

After a long talk about the convenience store incident, my mother went a step further in enlightening me. A week later, she took my brother and me to meet Sheriff John Baker Jr., a former player for the NFL's Pittsburgh Steelers. That's my favorite profes-sional football team and I was wide open to hearing what he had to say, until I realized he was planning to give us a tour of the Wake County jail.

Apparently, he knew more about me than I did about him. We toured a small part of the facility and then he introduced us to a cell of our own. We crossed the threshold, and behind us the bars closed with a creepy finality. *CLINK.* I never heard that sound be-fore or since.

Sheriff Baker spoke to us outside the cell, explaining how "life was changing," how "the neighborhood is changing," and the kids we've known forever "are not the same dudes anymore." He made it clear that we had to separate ourselves from the negativity. His huge hands grasping the bars, he looked me in my eye.

"You're not that type of kid," he said, his voice booming like a motorcycle engine.

I agreed with an embarrassed headshake. It was amazing how fast I shed my steely veneer. No more tough-guy routine. I had been a smart kid acting dumb. I vowed to change. From then on, it was school and sports. A locked cell has that kind of life-altering effect on a person. One can make a significant change in five seconds if motivated. I was completely motivated by the thought of spending my life in a crowded jail, smelling feces and urine, watching other men waste away.

"When they slam these gates, man ..." he said, pulling the bars open.

I was scared to death.

INSIDE THE

LOCKER ROOM

My mother used to tell us that to survive we needed book sense, street sense and common sense. If we used those senses together, we could make a reasonable choice despite the circumstances. It's simple logic I follow today.

I'd like to think that logic informed my decision to go home before my friends robbed a convenience store. I will never understand what guided me away. I'm blessed to be here without a police record. I don't judge my friends because I never consciously made the decision to not join them. God guiding my steps, I decided to watch TV, and I dodged a horrible fate.

We all make choices. Large or small, we're confronted with them every hour of the day. We typically base our decisions on long-term and short-term outcomes. I made stupid choices based on the short-term: *Do I steal something to wear to look better now or wait until I can afford it?*

I made wrong decisions because I wasn't comfortable with myself. I had one pair of jeans and one pair of shoes. And those were my everything shoes: for breakdancing, basketball and bike riding. I was insecure about my appearance. I thought I looked ugly, and having few clothes reinforced that feeling. Back then, girls wanted you to look like singer Al B. Sure and dress like Theo Huxtable from "The Cosby Show." I wasn't the dude guys wanted to be like, and I wasn't the guy the girls wanted. I thought: *Who am I? What good am I?*

That's a tremendous amount of self-applied pressure. I succumbed to peer pressure. Fortunately, I learned a great deal about myself from my "time" in jail. Most importantly, I learned who I was and who I wasn't.

CHALKBOARD

1. Stay True to You: I never expected regular people to understand me because I didn't consider myself regular. We are all bullied by peer pressure. Our friends can influence our thoughts and decisions, convincing us to make choices we otherwise might not make. But there are ways to avoid making choices that cross the line and place your life in jeopardy. Develop a creed. It may take time but think critically about rules that define your life. Write these rules down, clearly spelling out who you are and what you are about. With a creed, you create a list of principles that are nonnegotiable.

Once you write down the creed, you can always refer to the rules and add new ones. These rules will help guide you when you're faced with peer pressure. After you have adopted your creed, make your friends aware of what it says. Express your convictions and real friends will respect such a thought-out perspective. I don't smoke, drink or use drugs. At first, my friends laughed at me because I was an outcast, but over time they learned to respect my beliefs and didn't bother to ask if I wanted to indulge in that behavior. They laughed at me because I was different and I laughed at them because they were the same. Be yourself.

2. Avoid the Pack: A wise man once said, "Your net worth is the average of your five closest friends." Net worth doesn't necessarily equate to finances, but your overall character value. In my neighborhood, we rolled pretty deep. Depending on the day, there might be 15 of us riding our bikes to the basketball court. We didn't consider ourselves a gang or anything like that. We were outside playing. If we were thirsty, we rode our bikes to the corner store. No one was in charge, though the stronger personalities dominated and generally made choices for the group. This opened us all to some questionable decision-making, considering some of the dominant voices were cut-throat thugs. They made some shady choices. As a member of the group, one with his own voice, I often had to determine when it was time to break off from the pack.

For instance, I made an important decision when it was time to select a middle school. I was tired of traveling with the pack. Instead of enrolling in my district school, I convinced my mother that I'd get a better education at Daniels Middle School. I organized this change of venue myself, researching the school and application process. I presented my mother with the paperwork and she signed. This choice placed me in a new middle school without any friends or associates. I was one of the poorest kids in the school. The governor's son was in my seventh-grade class. Still, it was important that I set myself apart from old friends. I was comfortable with my friends but I knew I wanted the educational challenge and the experience of meeting new people.

3. Seek Advice: Somebody told me, "Really smart people do not have really good answers. They have really good questions." When in doubt, think it out. Consider every angle of the situation and compare the positives and negatives. Seek the advice of someone you trust outside of your friends. Perhaps this is a parent, sibling, neighbor, or teacher. Don't be afraid to ask questions. I've developed a "wise counsel" of individuals who provide me with honest insight and perspective when I have questions. They have helped my self-improvement and growth as I contend with life's challenges.

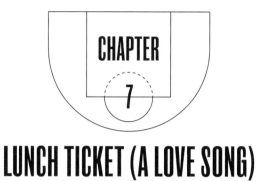

LUNCH TICKET (A LOVE SONG)

"Cause I need somebody, who will stand by me. Through the good times and bad times, she will always be right there for me. Sunny days, everybody loves them. Tell me baby, can you stand the rain?"
New Edition, "Can You Stand the Rain?" from "Heart Break"

SIDE A (LeVelle's Story)

Annisha Andrews broke my heart. She reached through my chest, grabbed my heart with both hands, threw it to the ground and smashed it with a sledgehammer, shattering it. She left me for dead in Lions Park. I never saw it coming.

We had been a happy couple. We were in love, the type of love that makes you doodle "Velle♥Nisha" in your notebook. She was my first love, my first real girlfriend. I met her through mutual friends in the neighborhood. I was a 15-year-old sophomore at Enloe High School and she was a 14-year-old freshman. She was good-looking, honey-brown with beautiful eyes and long hair. She smiled bright like Gabrielle Union. Skinny and self-conscious about my dark skin, I thought I was funny-looking. Still, I felt confident enough to talk to Annisha. Somehow we connected.

Over the course of a fabulous year, we were inseparable. From my apartment to her house was about a three-mile walk near Lions Park – a public park with baseball fields, tennis courts and playgrounds. Most days my walk felt like three minutes. I rode the bus to school in the mornings and then walked her home after school. I spent more time at her house than mine. My mother often called her house looking for me.

We talked all night on the telephone, our conversations about everything and nothing. *Who do you like better, Prince or Michael Jackson? New Edition or Jodeci?* We laughed at "In Living Color" and watched videos together. We stayed up way past "The Arsenio Hall Show." Half-asleep and fighting to stay awake, I'd hold onto the phone rather than hang up and wonder what she was doing. She made silence sound good.

Teenage love is powerful and spooky. It makes you do goofy, un-expected things. I led the varsity basketball team in scoring while we were together. She came to a game with her father, and I felt their presence in the gym. I tried too hard to impress them and had a terrible game. I was concentrating on her in the stands. Love is funny that way.

Annisha inspired me. When I went away for an AAU trip, I wrote her a 100-page letter. I wrote her letters all the time but never had I been so ambitious and expressive. I described everything we did on the trip. I wrote about how much I loved her. I jotted down songs lyrics. I plagiarized, borrowing from Luther Vandross, Babyface and other performers. I thought Lionel Richie was a hell of a writer. My mother played his "Can't Slow Down" album nonstop, and I knew every word. Mom's Motown collection was huge, so I borrowed from Smokey Robinson and Marvin Gaye. I poured my heart out.

We were a hot item and everyone knew. Annisha seemed happy. She held my hand while we walked. Our bond was so strong, our interests so intertwined, our passion so intense, I could have majored in her. My boys clowned me, but I shook their jokes off like a soap-soaked puppy. I was wet behind the ears yet determined to find out where this feel-good train was headed. Shakespeare could have written plays about our love affair, considering how it turned into a tragicomedy so quickly.

One day I was sitting in the cafeteria with Annisha when a bunch of seniors, friends of her older brother, circled our table. I knew from the devious smiles on their faces they weren't pulling up seats to chat about the weather. They were on a typical high school seek-and-destroy mission. Joke time had arrived. "What are you doing with this cat?" one guy asked Annisha. "Didn't you wear those jeans yesterday?" another guy asked me. These guys start cutting me up, laughing as if they were at a comedy club. It was friendly enough, but I was embarrassed on every level. I couldn't look at Annisha.

At Enloe, there were separate lines for lunch, one where you bought pizza and juice, and the other where you used a lunch ticket for your meal. With my mother's single-parent income, my lunch was completely subsidized by the state and my meals were free. I didn't even need to have my lunch ticket punched. These seniors knew the deal and started to clown my lunch ticket. "What is he going to buy you, he can't even buy lunch!" one of them said. I felt crushed, like in the scene in "The Nutty Professor" when Reggie, Dave Chappelle's character, clowned Sherman Klump – Eddie Murphy in the starring role – while he was on a date with Carla Purty, played by Jada Pinkett.

I turned to Annisha. She sat silent. Those seniors had ruined lunch.

When we walked from school together that afternoon, there wasn't much conversation. We got to the tennis courts at Lions Park, and Annisha had grabbed my hands. She told me she loved me, but "we're not going to be able to see each other any more." *Why?* She dropped my hands and headed up the hill toward her house, leaving me at the bottom of a hill. Rain soaked my clothes as I called after her. "Annisha!" She never turned around.

What started as a clear, sunny day had turned strangely cloudy. Thunder struck, the skies opened and rain poured. It was like a scene from the 1997 movie "Love Jones." Dejected and confused, I turned to make the longest walk of my life; it certainly felt like three miles. My face wet and my eyes bloodshot, I cried all the way home.

By the time I got there, Annisha was my ex-girlfriend.

She hadn't given me a reason why she broke up with me. I figured she was embarrassed by the lunch ticket jokes. The seniors had easily convinced my girl that I was financially worthless, and therefore, worthless overall. I stewed for the rest of the night. I cursed her name. I knew she was a good person and I didn't want to believe she was superficial, but the evidence pointed in the opposite direction. Perhaps she was shallow enough to break up with me over something someone else said. I couldn't believe what had happened.

My mother asked, "What is wrong?"

"Nisha broke up with me, and I think it was because she was ashamed of my lunch ticket," I said.

"Never allow anyone to dictate your worth," my mother said.

I gathered that message around me like a blanket.

Breakups come in phases. Initially you're heartbroken. Then you're sad. Then you're happy. Then you're dismayed. In the end, you're just mad, especially if you had no idea why you were dumped. I gave everything I had to Annisha and she dissed me.

I thought: Everyone I love disappeared, died or dismissed me. My father had left. My grandmother had died. And now my sweetheart had fled. I felt low.

I was through with love. I put on a coat of steel to shield me from heartbreak. I declared that no one was ever going to treat me that way again. I avoided Annisha for the next two years of high school. I walked into other buildings to avoid exchanging glances with her. I kept the lunch ticket as a reminder and as motivation to make a better life. *I've got to get out of here.* I was determined to get my family out of poverty. No one would mistake our circumstances in the future. Those jokes would not apply.

I keep material things as motivation, including my father's gift of a bicycle, which I never rode. My pride turns into stubbornness, and then I turn it into a game of motivation. I got it from my mother, who could hold a grudge like an underpaid employee. I keep things because I never want to accept what they represent again. When they tore down the original Orchard Park Houses, I asked a friend to collect dirt from the grounds in a cup. I never again want to live like we did in Orchard Park, so it was important that I kept soil from those grounds close to me. It may sound crazy, but you have to believe deeply in the vision you see for yourself.

Annisha exposed my vulnerability, and I didn't like that feeling. I was already shy about letting others into my world. I feared that if you loved someone and told everything about yourself, they would use it against you. I hadn't talked to anyone about my father until I shared my story with a girl I was dating. One day, she got mad at me and said, "So that's why your daddy left your black ass." Thank God for restraint.

Annisha committed the same crime in a different way. Her offense was so personal. I had built something very private with her, but at the same time very public. She carried around my dreams and goals. She knew my favorite colors and songs. I had hugged her mother, shook hands with her father and traded gibes with her younger sister. I was left to explain why we were no longer a couple and deal with people questioning me and meddling in my business. So yeah, I ducked and dodged her.

I had all the reminders I needed of Annisha. I kept that lunch ticket in my wallet for the next 26 years.

SIDE B (Annisha's Story)

There are always two sides to a story. Breaking up is difficult. I never wanted to leave LeVelle, especially the way I left him dumbfounded in Lions Park. He didn't deserve that.

We came together without much fanfare. Some friends in our neighborhood introduced me to him. Shy and unsure, I took easily to him. He was a nice guy. I mean a really nice guy, a polite gentleman who smiled freely and laughed and joked. He was clean-cut and handsome, always neat, if not the most stylish. I could tell he liked me. I liked him, too.

I knew kids in our neighborhood because of my brother, who was three years older. He was outgoing and knew everyone. I wasn't an outgoing person, though I managed to feel comfortable as a freshman because I knew my brother's friends. Enloe was my neighborhood school. My family had lived in Southeast Raleigh for three years, our backyard abutting Lions Park.

LeVelle and I started talking innocently enough and we got the nerve to start dating. When you're a teenager and you start to like someone, you're not thinking about anything else. What started as infatuation turned quickly into love. Suddenly, I was all head over heels. He used to say, "You're a pretty girl." I had the biggest crush on him. He was tall and skinny. The guys in my neighborhood would call him "Frail Velle," but that didn't bother me. They knew him from basketball. I didn't follow sports and didn't care that much about basketball. I only went to one game the whole time we dated. I didn't care that he was skinny or dark skinned – I liked his complexion. Dark chocolate. What stood out about him, what was truly attractive, was that he was respectable.

At the time, it was popular to date someone with light skin and curly hair – like the singer Al B. Sure. I didn't see looks. I had my own issues with beauty. How he treated me was most important. He walked me to class every single day. He lived quite a distance from me. Still, he walked to my house every chance he got. Rain or shine. I couldn't believe it.

We exchanged letters. He did better than most high school boyfriends. He was patient. He listened. He responded to my moods with understanding. He carried my books. I called it old-fashioned. I really liked that. For one, I didn't want to carry my own books. What girl does? He risked arriving late to class by walking me to my classroom. That's a selfless act you don't find with many young guys. His maturity impressed me.

LeVelle knew how to treat a girl. I remember we spent so much time talking on the phone. Looking back, it was ridiculous. My father arranged for a phone line in my room and I spent hours talking about music, artist, movies, television, school, family, everything and nothing. We did homework together on the phone. We fell asleep on the phone. There were many sleepy mornings as I headed to first period.

I'm not sure how LeVelle balanced our relationship with school and all of the other things, but he certainly had time to write. He went off on a basketball trip and I received a 100-page letter in the mail. That was crazy. I read it, too, every page. There were no pictures. He wrote about everything they accomplished; basketball drills, games won and loss and how much he was thinking about me.

Time passed and our relationship grew even more serious. People at school noticed how we were rarely apart. My girlfriends teased me. My parents commented, slipping in their thoughts when he dropped by after school. My mother generally had nothing but hugs and kisses for LeVelle. He was so courteous with his, "Yes, Mrs. Andrews." She ate that up. My father, however, wasn't so sure, his eyes closely following LeVelle when he sat on the couch. He said, "I don't mind you talking to the little skinny boy, but you're not concentrating on your school work." My grades were slipping. He said, "You need to get your priorities straight." He never said break up with LeVelle, but he kept telling me, "You have to do something." Talk less? I couldn't do that. I didn't want to make time for homework and studying like I was supposed to. I was more interested in talking on the phone.

No one, particularly a teenage girl in love, wants to listen to her parents, or acknowledge that they were right. But my dad was right. My grades dipped sharply. I got a "D" on a test. I was feeling the heat at home. At that age, even as an adult, when you love somebody, you want to spend all your time with that person. Because of our lack of maturity, we didn't know how to balance our feelings and responsibilities. Indeed, I had to do something.

So one day I wrote LeVelle a note and handed it to him in the hallway the following period, asking if he would walk me home. All the way to Lions Park, I kept thinking about how I was going to let him down. There were so many emotions flooding my body. I didn't say much at all as we walked. When we got to the base of the hill, which was like an alley adjacent to the park, I looked at him standing there. There was never going to be a comfortable moment to deliver my message, so I stopped stalling. I told him, "We can't continue to be together." He looked puzzled for a long time like *What are you saying?* He said, "What?" I didn't say anything more. I didn't tell him why.

When we arrived at the park, the sky was clear and it was a sunny day. Suddenly, though, the sky drew dark and soon it was raining. By the time I finished and turned away the rain was pouring. I was like, "Oh my God." He had to walk home in the rain.

Breaking up with LeVelle was hard for me. My actions went directly against what I was feeling. I loved him. He knew that. However, I needed to get myself together, readjust my priorities, improve my grades and most importantly, listen to my father. I walked away crying. I cried all the way home. I heard him calling my name, "Annisha!"

When I got home, I was a wreck. My sister said, "Why you making that ugly face." I explained to her that I had just broken up with LeVelle. Though she didn't like him, she understood the severity of the situation. We talked for a little while. I thought the feeling would pass, but I shuffled around for months disheartened and empty. I owed him an explanation, yet I couldn't call him or see him because that would send us right back to dating.

I had one serious boyfriend in high school after LeVelle and he didn't attend Enloe. I kept a low profile in school, eating lunch in the library or the hallway, and I didn't see LeVelle at all. After high school, I served in the military. I didn't throw away LeVelle's 100-page letter until I was in my late twenties and dating someone seriously. I kept it at my parents' house. I treasured the gesture. No one else had ever taken that much time to write me. Today I'm married with four kids and live in Greensboro. For years, I worked at a children's mental hospital. For six years, I've served as a volunteer advocate for abused and neglected children. I visit homes. I file court reports. I visit schools and foster homes. I serve as a child's voice in court.

This work is near and dear to my heart. Actually, too close. I was abused as a child, something LeVelle never knew. When I was 10, a family member beat me nearly beyond recognition. My aunt tried to kill me. I was in fifth grade. It's a story I've tried to forget.

My brother and I, along with my cousins, were at my grandmother's house in Warren County, N.C., for a party. All of the adults, except for my aunt, had left the house to prepare. They left us to play. My aunt, who we later discovered had a bad drug habit, separated me from the other children. I was so quiet that my brother didn't notice I was missing. The music was deafening. My aunt took me to a back room, locked the door and beat me bad. After a while, my brother and cousins noticed I was missing and busted down the door. My brother dragged her off me and someone called the police. He saw my face and said, "You look like the Elephant Man."

My mom, rest her soul, might have killed my aunt if her oldest sister hadn't intervened. They decided to handle the matter through the police, who ordered an arrest warrant. We took my aunt to court where she received five months probation for her actions against me. Meanwhile, I suffered a severely busted eardrum. Most of my scars were internal. Years later, before I entered the military, I discovered that my problems breathing while exercising were linked to the damage my aunt had done to my nose. Doctors had to break and reset my nose.

My aunt was high on drugs when she attacked me. I'm not sure if anyone knew the extent of her drug use. I am not sure why she singled me out. My injuries were so severe that when I arrived at the hospital, the doctor had to ask my mother to leave the room. They wanted to know who had struck me. My mom showed him paperwork from the police. As a 10-year-old, I testified in court to what happened. That was a scary moment, speaking in front of all those people, with my aunt staring me down. I was brave though and survived.

LeVelle had no clue what I had been through just four years before we dated. He had no idea that I felt ugly inside. I would have never made fun of him for what he looked like or for what he did not have. I was very sensitive to what I said to people because of my experiences. I didn't believe him when he said, "You are a pretty little girl." I loved him for saying it because it made me feel special. Sometimes as children, you're going through stuff, and your life is not all roses. I knew better than most LeVelle's situation and I would have never made light of it. Even with him thinking I broke up with him over a superficial lunch ticket, I cannot say one thing bad about him. He was a nice, respectful, attentive boyfriend. I think he was beyond his years. I still can't believe he was that way without a father in his life.

He was a gentleman all the way. I was very attracted to that. I didn't like the guys who seemed like trouble. I wanted someone down to earth. A regular guy. His mom did a really good job. He knew how to treat a girl.

INSIDE THE

LOCKER ROOM

I haven't seen Annisha in more than 26 years, but a couple of years ago, I received an email from her asking me to give her a call. I had no idea why she would contact me via email. What I heard over that phone was profound. "I just want you to know that my mother is sick and she doesn't have long to live," she said. "I know how you felt about her and I wanted to inform you of that."

My heart dropped.

What followed was something out of fiction. "Secondly, LeVelle, I owe you an apology!"

"An apology for what?" I asked.

"The day that I broke up with you."

"That's the past," I said.

She said the incident bothered her for a while. She described the afternoon in detail, recalling all the hurtful parts about the breakup. "Remember when I didn't turn around?" she asked.

"Yeah, I remember," I said.

"I was crying and I didn't want you to see me," she said. "I never wanted to leave you but I felt an enormous amount of pressure from my father."

Wow. I told her there was no need to apologize. I explained how I thought the breakup was because I needed a lunch ticket.

"I've kept it for over 20 years for motivation," I said.

Annisha has been an inspiration to me. I thought she broke up with me because I was poor, so I wanted to prove her and everyone else wrong. Every day I thought, "I'm going to give the world everything I got," and I worked with a chip on my shoulder. I maintained my cool even though I was angry, channeling my emotions into production. Before the breakup, I took 100 shots after basketball practice, but after the breakup, I starting taking 200. I walked around as though I could manage whatever someone threw at me. I found the inner voice that said You can do anything.

Motivation is a monster. Something has to inspire you to be successful, and it has to be consistent. I don't have an alarm clock anymore because I'm inspired to wake up and go. You can't sleep all day and live inspired.

You're going to experience distress but that shouldn't lead to self-destructive behavior. Inflicting pain on yourself or someone else because you're hurting is defeatist. Find another outlet. Bottle that pain and only release the cap while you're striving for something more significant. Use your steam to propel you forward. I could seat you in the Oval Office and invite President Barack

Obama, Oprah Winfrey, T.D. Jakes, Ray Lewis, Jay-Z and Beyoncé to talk with you about self-improvement and success. As gifted as they are – they could motivate snow to fall in summer – it would only help temporarily. Jay-Z isn't going to wake you up every morning and offer a breakfast pep talk. You'll never be successful until the voice that motivates you is your own.

CHALKBOARD

1. Pain is Motivation: Whether it's an impoverished childhood or a tumultuous relationship, there's always something to motivate you. Look to others for stories about what set them on the path to success and then build a blueprint for yourself. New England Patriots quarterback Tom Brady was motivated by his selection in the sixth round of the 2000 NFL Draft. Tyler Perry was motivated by his homelessness. I was motivated by a lunch ticket.

The smallest slight can remain with you for years. I used my breakup as one more thing that would help me reach my goals. I wanted to show my ex-girlfriend and anyone else who doubted me that I was destined to succeed no matter my living situation. I would do anything to help me focus on the task and deliver. Hold slights close to you, memorize every detail and recall them in tough times. That pain served as my motivation, because I never wanted to feel that emptiness again.

2. Make Tough Decisions: I have to applaud Annisha for breaking up with me. How many teenage girls would make the same decision? How many would listen to their fathers? Usually the young girl makes a decision based on emotion and remains in an unhealthy relationship in the name of love. She tries to hold on as long as possible, choosing her social life over priorities such as education and family.

Annisha listened to her parents and made herself miserable in the short term, yet she accomplished greater things later. She chose the future over instant gratification. That was a difficult decision. In hindsight, we were probably way too young and too serious to be that heavily involved. Although we were in love, our relationship distracted her from her education. She chose to eliminate the distraction.

3. Find True Love: All human beings desire to love and be loved. Whether you're two years old or 92, love affirms. It satisfies your desire to be appreciated. It stimulates your mind and allows you to grow. Once love is found, you feel an adrenaline rush beyond this world. I encourage you to find true love. Not someone who loves you because of looks, money or popularity, but someone who loves you despite your shortcomings.

CHAPTER

8

FIRST TIME

"Boys and girls in America have such a sad time together; sophistication demands that they submit to sex immediately without proper preliminary talk. Not courting talk — real straight talk about souls, for life is holy and every moment is precious."
Jack Kerouac, "On the Road"

W here I'm from, many males claim to first have had sex by age 12. They talk about the act as if they are experts, referencing their encounters in numbers so outrageous and preposterous that only a fool would believe them. "I've done it 100 times," someone might say. Neighborhood code says boys must front. They have to make up elaborate tales to prove machismo and impress friends who make up similar stories to appear cool and mature.

I was no different. I pretended I knew everything about sex. I talked to my friends as if I was a Kama Sutra instructor. I offered advice based on farcical conquests and made up elaborate tales to entertain my friends, regaling them with stories so vivid they belonged in romance novels. I'm certain someone along the way did say, "Stop lying." In truth, I knew only what I had seen on TV or overheard my older brother talking about among friends.

I was uninitiated until I was a freshman in high school. I had managed to remain cool despite severe urgings. My hormones were galloping like a horse at The Belmont Stakes, yet I wasn't chasing girls around the building trying to win races. Still, like a remote control, peer pressure can change your channel from ESPN to Playboy. One day after school, I stepped off the bus and my friend Dominique was waiting with a group of guys and girls. He invited us to his grandmother's house. "Nobody's home," he said.

There was a girl with the group I had never seen. She was visiting her cousin, who lived in our neighborhood. She smiled at me and I smiled back. My friends encouraged me to go after her, saying she was "ready." Before I knew it, we were alone in a dark room.

Usually I got out of this kind of situation before it reached this point. I was a master at fronting but when it came to doing, I was a neophyte. I fronted so hard about my sexual encounters, I put myself in an uncomfortable place – backed into a corner. What had I gotten myself into? I tried to use any excuse, including a lie about having sex the night before. Nothing worked. I tried to squirm my way out of it by saying, "I don't have any condoms."

Dominique knocked on the door and handed me a condom. I looked it over and noticed the creases and wear and tear on the package. *What is this?* This condom must have come from James Brown's wallet. Worn and tattered, the condom looked 30 years old. The wrapper was made from paper.

Among my friends, I was Don Juan. In that room, I was Don Cheadle. It was some of my best acting. Not only was the condom old, no one – notably my father – had instructed me on how to use one. I fumbled through the process and tried to be suave. We undressed in this dark room and I heard my friends gathered at the door, listening as if this was some type of peep show. Notice how quickly this house party became a freak show.

The girl and I got closer and finally engaged in sex. She was much more experienced than I was, though she didn't seem thrilled to be in the room. She, too, was a victim of peer pressure. I tried to make the event special, but as soon as I gained some familiarity and right as I started to climax, the condom burst. *What have I done?* We dressed and barely spoke to each other. She walked out of the room and told her cousin, "My stomach hurts." Her cousin looked me directly in the eye and said, "LeVelle, if she's pregnant, you're taking care of that baby."

What have I done? She walked out of the room five minutes after sex. *How could she be pregnant?* I walked the girl down the street to the bus stop and she said, "I think I'm pregnant." That was 10 minutes after sex. I was at a loss for words.

I walked home in the rain. I couldn't even enjoy the fact that I had just had sex. Drenched and tired, hungry and scared, I was consumed with the dread of some random girl being pregnant. That morning I had asked my mother to bring home Krispy Kreme donuts. A green and white box awaited me. I walked right by them. My mother was in the kitchen doing someone's hair. "Hey baby," she said. I whispered, "Hi" and kept walking to my room.

My mother said to her customer, "I'll be back, let me see what's going on with this boy." She came into my room. "What's going on with you?" I waited for a minute and then I said, "Ma, I did it."

"Did what?" she asked.

"You know."

She laughed without restraint, full and loud.

"No, no, no, this is real," I said.

"What?"

I explained the afternoon to my mother. She called Dominique's grandmother and everyone else involved, including my afternoon date. Our phone started ringing and she compared notes with other mothers. Dominique's grandmother's curses cascaded through the phone. "This ain't no whorehouse," she said.

What could I say? How could I ever ring her doorbell again?

I lived with anxiety about whether the girl was pregnant. I stayed in the house for a month. I hid like Osama bin Laden. My friends called the house: "Are you dead?" Mentally, I was gone. I tried to seek advice from people I trusted. Everyone said I'd be all right. I didn't believe them.

I hadn't heard from the girl in weeks. There was enough drama for a stage production. When my mother found out who the girl was, she shot me this look that said, "I wish you would bring her in here."

I visited the local pool hall, where I talked with Little Joe and Slick, my godfather. I felt unusually nervous and shy. "Boy, what's wrong with you?" I explained, but not exactly in private. I told my story in front of their homeboys – about 20 men in the pool hall.

"Well, I think I did it," I said.

"Boy, you got you some [stuff]?" Slick asked proudly.

"Man, that ain't funny," I said. "She says she pregnant."

"She pregnant?"

"Yeah, right after she said her stomach was hurting."

"Boy, that's 'cause you were tearing ...,"

Those guys were no help. I needed real information. So I visited the library and studied the science of a woman becoming pregnant. Researching like a pre-med major, I learned about a woman's menstrual cycle and human reproduction. More information just complicated the problem. I really thought I was going to be a teenage father.

Thankfully, she wasn't pregnant.

INSIDE THE

LOCKER ROOM

I almost fell into the booty trap. If you've never heard of the booty trap, then here's an explanation: A young man growing up in an urban environment has sex between the age of 16 and 23, choses not to use a condom, impregnates his partner and becomes a teenage father. Poor and without resources, living at home with his parents, this new teenage father chooses to take care of his responsibilities, but must accept a low-wage job because of his lack of education. Forced into a no-win situation, family pressure builds on his shoulders and he drops out of school. His child's mother soon drops out of school too. With limited education, they are stuck in the urban environment the boy so desperately wanted to escape.

It's a scenario few people address, and serious solutions are lacking. Yet it's a situation many young people face. Some manage to overcome the hardship and escape the trap, leaning on parents, grandparents and friends to help them through. Others face the situation and struggle. There's no way I was prepared to handle the responsibility of raising a child and heading a household. I was 15 and barely kept my room clean.

The ages 16 to 23 are critical. Good choices between those ages can equate to a good lifestyle for the remainder of your life. Make bad choices between those years and you are likely to struggle later on. There are exceptions but those are rare. A lot of boys, especially those in the urban ghettos, don't make it out after making a poor choice.

My first sexual experience scared me. I thought I had made a colossal mistake. By the time I reached college, I was so afraid of the booty trap I rarely sought sex from girls I dated. Girls thought I was the most respectful guy on campus because I never tried anything. I had worried myself into chivalry.

Around the time I entered my senior year, Earvin "Magic" Johnson announced he had contracted the HIV/AIDS virus from unprotected heterosexual sex. I became even more uncertain about sex. That was enough to keep me in the gym at night shooting basketballs.

CHALKBOARD

1. Abstain: Don't engage in sex if you're not mentally ready to handle the day-after-sex experience. There's no need to rush. Ignore peer pressure to try anything you can't confidently talk with a parent or doctor about. Resist peer pressure by talking to others who are contemplating the same choices. Support each other. Join groups that support your decision.

2. Visit a Home for Teenage Mothers: Peer pressure among teens is impairing our community. Boys and girls are equally fallible in this regard, listening to their hormones instead of common sense. Think about the outcome of a negative experience every time you consider engaging in sex. Investigate different outcomes of random sexual encounters, particularly where no protection is used. Educate yourself about babies. Try babysitting. Spend several hours with a baby when you are responsible for watching, feeding, clothing and changing diapers. Count how much free time you have from the time you start until you finish. You might think twice about how much responsibility you want and how much you can reasonably handle.

For a more advanced experience, find a social service program in your community that helps teenage
mothers transition in life. Visit a teen mom, befriend her
and ask to shadow her for a week. Monitor her week
closely, looking at her schedule. How does she handle
transportation, day care, food, shelter, employment and
education for herself and the baby? How has her life
changed? Who helps her? How often does she get a
break? How often does she see friends? Ask many more
questions and learn as much as you can about her life.
Then place yourself in her shoes and ask yourself: Could
I comfortably walk in her shoes?

3. Protect Yourself: The obvious meaning here is use
protection – a condom or some form of approved pre-
vention found in your local drugstore – if you are going
to engage in sexual activity. If you are sexually active,
monitor your health and get tested for sexually trans-
mitted diseases frequently. Demand that your partner
get tested.

Protecting yourself, however, extends to decision-
making. Do the math before making short-term decisions. Can you afford a child? Calculate a year's worth
of diapers, even buying the cheap brand. Purchasing a
box of diapers four times a month at $25 each will cost
$1,200 a year. Add milk. Add food. Add toys. Can you

afford these items on minimum wage? Then research
the cost of daycare.

CHAPTER
9

PLAYGROUND LEGEND

*"I wasn't the bad person
everybody thought I was."*
Raleigh, N.C., native Gary Mattison

very neighborhood nominates a future NBA Hall of Famer, a
would-be Michael Jordan. It recognizes the talent at an early age
and declares his stock will rise far beyond that of a playground
legend. It mentally measures his arms, legs and feet, projecting his
potential height and raving about it in barbershops. It watches him
grow, full of milk he drank at his grandmother's table. It marvels at
his preternatural skills as he dribbles with the ease of a breeze. It nur-
tures his development with a forearm to the back and heavy-handed
fouls at the lip of the hoop. It feeds his ego with yelps of "I see you,"
every time he pours in a jump shot like wine from a decanter.

My neighborhood nominated Gary Mattison.

We watched him grow into a phenomenal young ballplayer we
believed had the God-given gifts to excel in college and the NBA. We

cheered him, just knowing he could be the first from Lane Street to make the big-time. We expected him to shine on the grand stage next to then-NBA commissioner David Stern, make a shipload of money during an illustrious career, retire and bring some of his superstardom back to the neighborhood. We watched Los Angeles' Earvin "Magic" Johnson and Boston's Larry Bird on television, but we saw Gary Mattison in person. There's no way, we imagined, either of them had been as good as Mattison at age 15.

Gary Mattison was my hero, older than me by six years. We met at the basketball court when he was playing with my brother Verne. When you're a kid, your older brother is like the Incredible Hulk. You think nobody is stronger or faster. Every sport I played, I tried because of my brother. This was especially true of basketball because I had been more talented in baseball and football. As my brother hit his teens, he developed into a natural power forward on the court, his body thicker and heavier than mine. I was slim as an iPhone. I couldn't emulate him anymore.

My brother often played with Kevin and Steven Jones, who lived a block behind us. I figured Kevin, Steven and my brother were the best on the court, but during one game at the Raleigh Boys & Girls Club, they kept deferring to a tall, slender guy I'd never seen before. He took their passes and netted 20 points before anyone blinked. It was as easy for him as swallowing. Who in the hell is this dude? Over time, we were all introduced to Gary Mattison.

He lived with his grandmother and three sisters in a neighborhood called Mayview, a good ways away from the Boys & Girls Club. Who put a basketball in his hands? God is the answer. Once he picked the ball up, he rarely put it down. He couldn't reach the courts fast enough. He was a little guy attending Sherwood-Bates Elementary School. "I used to come home and throw my books in the floor and just go to Jaycee Park," Mattison said. He clocked hours in front of the TV, watching Julius Erving, aka Dr. J, destroy the competition in the American Basketball Association before it merged with the National Basketball Association after the 1975-76 season.

Others were watching and betting on his athleticism. Mattison seldom visited the Boys & Girls Club, where I was a "club kid," dropped off every summer morning and there through the evening. Mattison came sporadically, but when he came, though, he drew attention. Ron Williams remembers watching Mattison lead his baseball team to a city championship as a nine-year-old pitcher. He recalls attending a party at a friend's house and seeing Mattison play basketball. "He was a phenomenal athlete," he said, "but had no parental guidance." Mattison's parents, Mary Gibbs and Tom Mattison, were divorced. Mattison stayed with his grandmother, Dorothy Jenkins, who nurtured him and his sisters, Nita, Tammy and Regina.

Mattison attended my middle school – Daniels – where to his surprise he was cut from basketball tryouts as a seventh-grader. Bob Sandford, who was a close friend of North Carolina basketball great "Pistol" Pete Maravich, coached the team and chose his roster. "I guess my talents wasn't good enough at the time," said Mattison, who was 5-foot-7-inches at the tryout.

That summer Mattison grew two inches. He made the team as an eighth grader. His newfound height was a sure advantage.

Mattison's talents made him a target of competitive coaches. He played for Williams at the Boys & Girls Club when he was 12, but his former basketball coaches tried to persuade him back to their squads with ice cream and candy. That was only the start of people trying to manipulate Mattison and use his athletic talents. We all saw it.

Steven Jones was a point guard on many of the basketball teams with Mattison, including an All-Star team at the Boys & Girls Club. "We'd just tell the scorekeeper, 'Go ahead put 35 or 40 in the book, he's gonna get that. Go ahead and mark that down.'" Jones said

Mattison was fun to play with because he scored, was unselfish, and was a cool guy, even when he started distancing himself from the fellas at the club. Mattison was a year older than Jones, but they were close. He called his point guard "Twin" because he looked so much like his brother Kevin.

When Mattison wanted your attention, he'd whistle loud as a freight train down the block. Few sounds outside police sirens could cut through a crowd like his whistle. I envied his whistle because I couldn't whistle at all.

Bright-eyed and enthusiastic with his gas tank always full, Mattison grew taller and improved as a basketball player. He credits his sisters with making him tough and competitive. Both Nita and Tammy played basketball at Broughton High School. They tortured him before he could stand on his own. "They used to beat me up and everything," Mattison said. "It made me better." He suffered defeat in many one-on-one contests before he could command bragging rights with his sisters. Things changed when he reached 14.

Suddenly, he sprouted to about 6-foot-2, towering over his sisters. Confident and skilled, he challenged them to a game of one-on-two and won. "I started beating both of them together," he said. "That's how I got real good."

As an eighth grader, he played pick-up games at N.C. State, his top college choice. Facing college players like Dereck Whittenburg, Chucky Brown, Brian Howard, Lorenzo Charles and Rodney Monroe, Mattison developed at a rapid pace. His talent, like a wealthy man in a bull market, only grew richer. "I used to do stuff that surprised myself," Mattison said.

"He could do it all," Williams agreed. Mattison entered Broughton High School and helped the baseball team reach the N.C. High School Athletic Association state championships. From that point, his reputation exploded in our neighborhood. He leveraged his athletic gifts for attention and status. Girls started to notice him. Guys admired his cool. Yet he remained one of the nicest, most kind-hearted people.

We recognized Mattison as a talent but questioned where he'd end up.

"He didn't have the right influences in his life," said Williams, who knew Mattison's father and spoke with him about the problem. "I said, 'Look, your son gonna be good, man. ... You need to put your hands on that little boy. You need to take control.'"

Mattison moved at his own pace. He made his own rules. He roamed the neighborhood.

I let Mattison know I admired his game. Michael Jordan helped North Carolina to a NCAA Tournament championship in 1982, but I didn't know him. N.C. State guard Dereck Whittenburg was helped the Wolfpack to a NCAA Tournament championship in 1983, but I didn't know him. I knew Mattison.

I watched him play pick-up at the mini-park. He was a smooth, powerful dude on that basketball court. He did everything with purpose and his shot was effortless. I chose basketball over baseball and football partly because of the way Mattison played.

Mattison gave us hope. He was the first guy from our neighborhood I remember people saying had a chance to make it. My neighborhood had had only eight people go to college in 35 years. Mattison, like New Edition, motivated me with his gifts. We believed he could make it out of the ghetto and cross over to a wonderful life.

So we cheered Mattison, No. 44, as a member of Broughton High School's varsity basketball team. He didn't play much as a junior, for academic reasons. Coach Marshall Hamilton had a reputation as a disciplinarian and he set strict team rules. Broughton was known for high academic achievement and challenging coursework. There were few shortcuts for students and even fewer for student-athletes. "Marshall's attitude was that you can be my star player but you're not going to get any more special treatment than anyone else," said Jeff Gravley, who covered Broughton as a reporter for WRAL-TV in Raleigh. "I think that helped Gary immensely."

In the neighborhood, we overlooked Mattison's academic troubles. School never came easy for him. "I did as much as I could," he told me. "It wasn't like I wasn't trying. I just couldn't. It just wasn't for me." He said he didn't learn what he was supposed to at an early age and that placed him behind other students. With his parents divorced, and him living with his grandmother, his elementary education fell through the cracks. "That really messed me up," he said.

"They're trying to teach me how to read and how to do all this stuff at 13 years old," he continued. "That's why they say, 'He don't know nothing, he's dumb.' That's how they did me." He said his mother, father and sisters tried to help him once they realized how good he was at sports. It was too late.

"Y'all should have been showing me," Mattison said. "But they had to really teach themselves. ... It was hard to show me – the little one – and they don't really know themselves. But namely I just tried to learn stuff by seeing it. I'd see stuff on the billboard and try to pronounce it." He said he never really got a good grasp of reading until he was older and started studying on his own.

As much as Mattison struggled academically, he flourished on the basketball court as a senior. Hamilton restricted him to three quarters per game. He came off the bench in the second quarter. That didn't seem to bother him as much as it bothered the crowd, which often roared, "Put Gary in."

Mattison's offensive outbursts were extraordinary. He'd come off the bench and knock down 30 points. High school basketball players only play eight-minute quarters, so the amount of work he put in during 24 minutes boggles the mind. He commanded the ball but never begged for passes or took ill-advised shots.

"He's the same kind of player that Scottie Pippen was," Williams said referring to the former NBA star. "He could shoot it; he could put it on the floor."

The late N.C. State coach Jim Valvano took notice of Mattison as a 10th-grader during a holiday tournament at Broughton. Valvano was there to see Charles Shackleford, a player for Kinston who had signed with N.C. State. Kinston tipped off against Broughton and both players started performing. Shackleford dunked. Mattison dunked. Valvano began the game sitting next to Shackleford's mother, but then he moved. "By the time I ran back down the court, he was sitting over there with my mom," Mattison said.

I remember Valvano coming to our neighborhood, outside of the mini-park, to recruit Mattison. He wore red and laughed a lot. We knew Mattison was loyal to State and this only stamped the deal in our minds.

For all he had accomplished, Mattison made his name in the 1986 NCHSAA 4-A high school state championship game against West Charlotte. I attended that game with Nate McMillan's nephew, Dominique, whose father drove us. McMillan, a standout from Raleigh, would later star as a point guard for N.C. State and the NBA's Seattle Supersonics. The game was at the University of North Carolina's Dean Smith Center, at that time in its first year of operation. Broughton High School is about a 20-minute ride from Chapel Hill, where the game was held. But as far as you could see into the crowd there were people wearing Broughton purple and gold. The whole neighborhood, it seemed, came out to support Mattison.

Coach Hamilton, tall and stern, held firm and kept his star player on the bench for the first quarter of the game. The crowd yelled, "Put Gary in." West Charlotte, which boasted a 28-0 record, went ahead 10-0 to start. At the start of the second quarter, Mattison checked into the game and reeled off five straight buckets. "And, when I say them brothers were playing defense, they were right here," Jones said, demonstrating a hand in a defender's face.

Once Mattison was in the game, the teams traded baskets in a close contest. There were seven lead changes in the fourth quarter. West Charlotte had four players finish in double figures, as 6-foot-2 senior forward Cliff Caldwell led the team with 16 points. He scored two points in the final 1 minute 30 seconds to lift his team to a 67-66 victory. Broughton missed a shot at the buzzer that could have won the game.

Mattison scored 33 points and was named MVP. His team loses and he takes home most valuable player. Only Mattison.

Basketball season ended and that championship game closed the chapter on Mattison's high school career. He said he graduated with a 1.9 grade point average. He did not qualify academically to attend N.C. State as a freshman and so he enrolled at Chowan Junior College in Murfreesboro, N.C.

Junior college provided a clean slate for Mattison. Beginning on the bench in his first semester, his talents won over Coach Bob Burke, who inserted him into the starting lineup. He fit like a plug in a socket, averaging 18.3 points per game during the 1986-87 season. He was the first Chowan freshman named to the All-Region team. He signed a letter of intent to play at N.C. State for Valvano.

Mattison made an indelible mark on the junior college ranks. Burke called him the best shooter/scorer he ever coached, a list of future Division I collegiate athletes and professionals including McMillan.

"He could stop on a dime and shoot. It's a very difficult skill," Burke said. "He knew how to drive and get in between gaps. He had a great sense of knowing when to take it all the way in or when to not challenge."

"Very soft-spoken," Burke said about Mattison. "Never gave me a problem."

But he gave opponents hell. The NCAA introduced the 3-point line to college basketball in his freshman year and Mattison took advantage with his sweet jump shot.

Terrence Ross, from New Bern, went to Craven Community College in fall 1987. The 6-foot-2 off guard, known as a defensive specialist, played two seasons at Craven Community and faced Mattison several times. The scouting report had named Mattison the player to watch, but that struck Ross as odd when he watched Chowan warm up. He was not impressed.

"Gary was one of those types where you could see him always laughing, playing with the guys, just dribbling around," Ross said. "You can't really find out how he can play because with the way he was playing around."

Then the game started. Ross saw a quiet guard able to manage the team and game tempo.

"Gary was like one of the most complete guards that I've seen through the history of basketball," Ross said. "That's not an understatement."

Mattison was solid, played with a nonchalant virtuosity and "he had an instinct for the game," Ross said. "I call it a quiet storm." He knew the floor and he knew his position, in a way similar to the style of Los Angeles Lakers' Earvin "Magic" Johnson. "He could score when he wanted," Ross said. "He could get an assist when he wanted. He could get a rebound when he wanted. He could basically just do what he wanted.

"When he had the ball," Ross said, "you were at his mercy."

After two years playing for Burke, Mattison left junior college as a Division I honorable mention All-American in 1989. He did not graduate from Chowan. He planned to play for N.C. State, spending off days playing pick-up games with State players and, he said, visiting Valvano at his home. "I was grinding as hard as I could at studies to try and get that biology and that English that I needed to get," Mattison said.

Despite giving his best, he still did not qualify for enrollment at N.C. State, failing to secure English and biology credits he needed.

For a player like Mattison, who struggled with academics, it was the worse possible time to join the N.C. State basketball program. A major scandal involving the program had taken over the front pages of local and national newspapers. Former students and staff accused some athletic department staff of academic fraud and pay-for-play. A scathing book, "Personal Fouls – The Broken Promises and Shattered Dreams Of Big Money Basketball At Jim Valvano's N.C. State" spelled out the controversy. The accusations sparked an NCAA investigation that led to Valvano leaving the program.

Valvano said "don't even come because it might mess you up,'" Mattison said. He had no choice but to move on.

The NCAA in 1986 adopted Proposition 48, which stipulated minimum high school grades and standardized test scores student-athletes must have before enrolling in college. It required the completion of a 16-core course, and there was a sliding scale requirement that matched grade-point average and standardized test scores.

Without adequate grades in English and biology, there was no chance for Mattison to earn an associate degree, and thus there was no chance for him to enroll at N.C. State. He chose his second-best offer, enrolling at St. Augustine's College, where he knew the late coach Harvey Heartley, Sr., from youth summer camps. He transferred to an NCAA Division II college without penalty and played in the Central Intercollegiate Athletic Association. "He came in December and the rest is history," said Heartley, who met Mattison as a seventh grader and give him basketballs and scholarships to his basketball camp, hoping one day he might get to coach the slim boy with man-size talents.

Mattison played point guard and wing at St. Augustine's College. "Everybody knew he had it," Heartley said. "He could shoot the

3-point shot standing flat. He could pass or shoot, then if you came up on him, he would go around you."

Mattison averaged more than 40 points in his first six games. He played 47 games in two years, averaging 45.9 percent from the field and scoring 25.8 points per game. He shot a career 44.7 percent from 3-point range and averaged 4.4 assists per game. During his senior season, he averaged 29.4 points per game, and at several times throughout the season led the nation in scoring. The Falcons relied on him for instant offense and he scored in bunches. He finished his career at St. Aug's with 1,211 points.

Talent draws attention. And word quickly spread about St. Aug's high-scoring guard. NBA scouts from the Seattle SuperSonics, Washington Bullets, Chicago Bulls, Philadelphia 76ers, Atlanta Hawks and others flooded the school's bandbox gymnasium to watch Mattison perform.

Academics were more challenging.

"I wouldn't say it was hard for him, but he didn't put his attention on his class work and going to school as he should have," Heartley said. "I had him a tutor. All Gary wanted to do was play basketball."

"St. Aug's assistant coach Rick High called Mattison "very high maintenance. For him to go to class, we had to go to class." High grew up around Mattison and said when others were home studying, Mattison was outside playing basketball. Mattison never developed the study habits needed to compete academically, he said.

I took advantage of the chance to watch Mattison at St. Aug's, which was walking distance from my family's apartment. I attended coach Heartley's summer camps and watched the college teams practice. By his senior season, Mattison had reached his zenith as a college basketball player.

The neighborhood supported Mattison, although he was better off without some of the people in his life. His raw talent made some envious. We all thought the NBA was a foregone conclusion. We saw the scouts at the games. We saw the box scores in the newspapers.

But there was more to the process than simple stats. The NBA is an exclusive club. Its executives are careful about whom they invite to participate. Mattison said his paperwork to participate in the 1991 annual NBA pre-draft combine was never completed by a St. Augustine's College coach. Players undergo a series of tests over the course of several days to determine strengths and weaknesses. There are strength and skill drills, as well as five-on-five play. Team scouts evaluate players to help organizations make decisions about draft selections. Players who perform well are either drafted by NBA teams or invited to preseason training camps with a chance to earn a roster spot.

The NBA combine is a big deal for Division II fringe prospects like Mattison. For much of the season, they play in front of small crowds, without national television cameras showcasing their talents. Some scouts visit their games but not always. The combine provides the platform for players to strengthen their positions and somehow, go from unknown to known overnight based on their performance on a large stage. Dunk on a top draft prediction and perhaps another team may take notice. The opportunity is serious and not to be taken for granted. He never had a chance to display his gifts.

That hurt my heart. I was pulling for Mattison. This is where his life veered off target and he was unable to fulfill his dreams.

The Charlotte Hornets selected Larry Johnson as the top pick in the 1991 draft. Two N.C. State players were chosen in the second round: Rodney Monroe was taken 30th overall by Atlanta and Chris Corchiani was taken 36th by Orlando.

Mattison was selected by the Sioux Falls Skyforce as the 126th pick overall in the 1991 Continental Basketball Association Draft. He was waived in training camp and never appeared in a regular season game. He later played in Santo Domingo, Dominican Republic. "I didn't get a chance to go to no camp," Mattison told me. "I wish I could have."

Heartley, who died on June 23rd, 2014 after a bout with cancer, described Mattison "as the kind of boy you want as a player." He saw the bright side in his All-American. High, though, saw both sides. He said the coaching staff was never given clarification about why Mattison didn't participate in the NBA combine. "He wasn't ready," High said. "He wasn't ready socially."

Mattison, who takes some responsibility for his actions, particularly later in life where he made poor choices that led to several arrests, said he has never understood what happened to his chance at superstardom. He says his reputation was tainted along the way, with rumors of drug use. The image was impossible to shake, he said, and discouraged scouts and others from taking a serious interest in him. He denies serious drug use, though he admits he used drugs like marijuana as a teenager. When he was playing basketball in college he was drug-free, he says.

When Mattison returned from a year playing in Santo Domingo, he says, he didn't know how to continue his career. He had few professional connections and even fewer resources to help him land an NBA tryout. He gave that dream up and tried to clear his name. "How was I going to get my name back straight? I knew that when I left here my name was kind of dragged through things," he said. "They were saying that I was getting high, I was using drugs, I was drinking and all.

"I wasn't the bad person people thought I was."

Mattison said it took six years to rebuild an acceptable reputation in the neighborhood where people identified him as a person and not a drug user. "I just wanted to find myself," he told me. "The only way I could find myself was to be by myself."

He worked odd jobs and pulled himself together. Still, he wasn't comfortable. He was haunted by the stigma of drug use and made an unusual decision. He started selling drugs in 2003. "Everybody was saying that's what I'm doing, so I say, 'Hey,'" Mattison said. "'I know everybody who's doing it. So I might as well do that to get myself established. Then once I got myself established, I kind of slid away from it."

Over the years, he gravitated to and away from drugs, finding trouble with the law and serving time in jail on numerous occasions. He continued to teach himself to read and participated in skill-development courses. He sought jobs, landing some, losing others, and never quite finding a real place in society.

"As far as living comfortable, no I'm not comfortable," he told me. "I'm living day-by-day."

For many college students, the transition from campus to the professional world is daunting. Some find a job, others move back home. His dreams unfulfilled, Mattison found an alternative by heading overseas to play for an international team.

In the end, his life was hard to watch. He never found NBA stardom. He struggled to survive, abusing drugs and landing in jail. He's turned his life around to a degree – a hard task for a felon – but still searches for the promise of that bright-smiling boy who used to whistle like a freight train.

INSIDE THE

LOCKER ROOM

Outside of his family, I was Mattison's biggest fan. He'd see me and say, "What's up Lil' Velle." I felt special. I always wanted him to succeed and to work in the NBA. If he could make it, those of us behind him could also. His life was like a case study for me – good and bad.

I stole from his collection of offensive moves. I mimicked his smoothness. In college, I picked up the nickname, "Poetry 'n Moton," but it was Mattison whose game read like Nikki Giovanni to me. His life also read like poetry, replete with lines of caution and tales of woe.

Mattison was the first guy to convince me that God gives you talent, but it's your responsibility to maintain that talent. He was given a combination of choices that needed to be made correctly. For whatever reason, he made bad choices and paid for them when it counted.

I felt devastated when Mattison didn't get into N.C. State. Everyone knew how badly he wanted to attend. We remembered Valvano smiling in the hood, recruiting him. I learned a valuable lesson about education and finally grasped why it was necessary. People were telling me I was next, and I didn't want to be denied any opportunity. I was determined to leave the ghetto and improve my mom's quality of life.

Prior to that, I listened when teachers spoke about the value of education but it didn't make practical sense. I thought you played basketball until you became a millionaire and then you died. In reality, the basketball stops bouncing, if you're lucky, around 35. If you are extraordinarily lucky, you make millions. I understood the value of having educated people around me and making sure they had my best interest at heart.

When Gary Mattison failed to get into N.C. State, there were rumbles around the neighborhood, some people laughing at his academic shortcomings. It wasn't funny. I felt for the guy because I knew him. Different from many star players, Mattison was a good dude, easygoing and likable. He had a kind spirit. He didn't wish anyone harm. He didn't harm anyone but himself. I rooted for him without regret but people turned on him.

It's hard to believe Mattison once had groupies. But he doesn't have those anymore because he didn't go pro. He can't shoot the ball and make people feel good. He can't shoot the ball and make money. His so-called friends have disappeared. By watching him, I learned a great deal about how to judge real friends.

I learned from watching Mattison that there's always a need for transition, especially if basketball doesn't become all that you thought it might. I never played in the NBA, and I had some success in international competition. I knew, though, when it was time to come back home. I became a teacher and a coach and haven't looked back. I had a strong support system and used basketball to leverage contacts for my life. I had strong advisers help me make decisions. I listened to my mother and her advice.

Mattison's life was like a HBO dramatic TV series. You tune in every week to keep up with the characters. You can't turn the channel. And by mid-season, everyone's talking about how they think the series will end.

Mattison's finale disappointed me, yet the dialogue was rich. Listen closely to what Mattison says about his desire for a better education. If you take anything from his story, note his unfortunate mis-education. His words are there to serve as a beacon to those traveling in similar choppy waters.

CHALKBOARD

1. Take Responsibility: While there are major problems with our country's education system, everyone has the opportunity to obtain a free public school education. That means you have been promised a basic education by birthright. Acquire a basic understanding of reading, writing, math, science and history. Take it upon yourself to acquire as much as you're capable of acquiring. Your parent or guardian should insist, especially during your elementary years.

If they don't, advocate for yourself. Show up to school, go to class, engage in the work placed before you and complete it. Go home and complete your homework. Study. Ask questions. Learn something you don't like. Few people love school, but it's your job until you replace it with a profession. Nothing is more important.

Master your basics and demand that someone help you comprehend what you don't understand. Take your education into your own hands. Place as much energy in your lessons as you might a hobby, sport, video game or romantic relationship. Actually compare how much time you spend studying versus hanging with friends.

If you text more than you study science, you may have problems with science.

Stay late at school. If you demand help and stay to receive it, someone will help you. If you grasp the basics, life becomes easier and you have a better chance of becoming a productive citizen. No one says you have to be perfect or the smartest in your class, but if you put in the effort, you will acquire the skills necessary to survive in America.

2. Plan B: Education is the key to success and longevity. I come across so many people who desire to have a career in sports or entertainment, as either a basketball player or rapper. I wholeheartedly encourage you to pursue your dreams but understand that career expectancy in those fields is an average of five years. After one's singing career has ended, singers are usually ill-prepared for what they face the rest of their lives. They may be 25 and have not planned for a future without sports or entertainment.

You need an alternative plan if you choose any sports or entertainment field because of the high turnover rate. Please remember: The ball will stop bouncing and the camera will stop flashing. When your moment is over, you must have a secured foundation of education to make the transition into the real world a successful one.

If you're not interested in scholarship, create a backup plan for your life and career choice. What do you want from life? What if that doesn't work out? What's next? Think through your first career plan all the way to a successful ending. Then think through the same career scenario with an unsuccessful ending. How would you rebound? What are your other interests? Do those interests translate to interesting career choices? Have you honed those skills? What does it take to sharpen them? Are you prepared to change direction?

3. Close Circle: Surround yourself with good people who care about you and not just about what you do. Life around the game of basketball has become cynical. The fundamental morals and values the game once taught have been replaced by lucrative business and vultures that prey on kids' abilities for financial gratification. That's not to say one size fits all, but there are some who take advantage of the weak and ignorant. Think about this. Basketball is one of the few sports that people can coach or train players when they've never played the game.

I can't train a 12-year-old golf prodigy to become the next Tiger Woods, or coach a 15-year-old boxer to become the next Floyd Mayweather Jr. Their parents would question my qualifications from the start.

But families nowadays have allowed outsiders to be the primary consultants for their child in basketball-related matters. The problem is that these people have ulterior motives and are seeking long-term paydays. Not only have they ruined the sport, they have fooled families into believing they are concerned about the kids' general welfare.

Keep your circle tight. Don't allow outsiders into the picture. My mother was uneducated about the game of basketball, but had a Ph.D. in recognizing someone trying to take advantage of her child.

CHAPTER

10

SOMEBODY PRAYED FOR ME

*Somebody prayed for me, had me on their
mind. Took the time and prayed for me.
I'm so glad they prayed ... I'm so glad they
prayed ... I'm so glad they prayed for me*
gospel hymn "Somebody Prayed for Me"

My inner fool agreed to play basketball for Coach Frank Williams at Enloe High School. There were other options. Coaches throughout the region had been recruiting me in middle school to play for their teams, assuring me of how much playing time I would receive, enticing me with how many points I could score. Williams never called, sent a message or even winked.

His disinterest intrigued me. I wanted to play for someone who would make me earn every start. Self-reliant and cocksure, I didn't want anyone to give me anything. As they say, be careful what you ask for. I enrolled at Enloe High in 1988 to find that our basketball coach had previously dismissed the team's best player for arriving at tryouts one minute late. I didn't believe that until I met Coach Williams. I had never met anyone like him.

Coach Frank Williams micromanaged every detail. He covered every angle. There was a precise way he had our team practice. There was a uniform way he expected players to dress. There was a standard of behavior he expected. He demanded a high level of fitness. He was a stickler for decorum and time.

Often Coach Williams required us to begin practice at 6 p.m. If you showed up at 6:01, you were late, and late arrivals need not show at all. The doors were closed. Eventually, after we learned the rules, we showed up an hour early to ensure we wouldn't be late.

"I only did what I felt in my heart needed to be done to train you guys to be young men in the future, to discipline you guys when you were doing things wrong," he told me.

Coach Williams walked the hallways like there was an emergency, his stride heavy and swift. Brawny like a bodyguard or pro wrestler, he stood 6 foot, 4 inches tall. He would lift weights at school and change into a sleeveless T-shirt that revealed bulky arms swollen against his sides. He was hard as a correctional officer with twitchy eyes daring you to misbehave.

He was a radical disciplinarian. How many basketball coaches make players wear skirts during practice? He kept two colorful skirts with the equipment – one a mini-skirt, the other an Olivia Newton-John in "Grease" pleated skirt. If you violated team rules – and there was a list of rules as long as a legal pad – you wore a skirt during practice. Unlike college teams, we had open practices, and the cheerleaders and the dance teams were in the same gymnasium. Everyone watched you complete shooting drills in Jordans, a tank top and a skirt. Try explaining that.

When I received an in-school suspension for acting out in class, Coach Williams made me wear a frilly skirt to practice. I practiced my butt off in that skirt, even though I felt humiliated and embarrassed. I never wanted to wear it again.

"I had to do things back then to get your attention," Coach Williams explained to me recently. "My point was for you to focus. And I guess it was to embarrass because we were embarrassed."

Others had to carry bricks to class after games. If you missed a shot hard off the iron rim, that was called shooting a brick. If you shot too many bricks during a game and finished with a low shooting percentage, you carried a brick to class. Coach Williams wanted everyone to use proper form, follow-through and shoot near 70 percent.

"All of the fundamentals were extremely important to me," he said. "And sometimes the kids would tease them, their friends. So you know how strong peer pressure is? Those kids know when they see that brick you have shot a brick in the game. You don't want to go through that again."

Though the coach spread his authority equally, I was a consistent target. I was the best player and the team leader, he later told me, so he set an example by leaning hard on me. From my freshman season until I graduated, he was inflexible and unappeasable. He yelled and fussed, demonstrating his point with an iron-clad ferocity that let the team know there was no room for foolishness. He preached team basketball and demanded physical preparedness.

One night I scored 57 points at Cary High School, which had become a personal rival. Some Cary students found out I lived near the Lane Street projects and yelled as a group, "food stamps" during introductions. They taunted me during warm-ups and saw that it bothered me, so they increased their tyranny. I missed my first two shots but finished the night on fire, prompting a standing ovation.

After the game, a newspaper reporter asked how I felt. I talked about how good it felt to score so many points in a rival gym. With little regard for my teammates, I praised my own performance and spoke about my intentions.

The next day, the local newspaper had a story on the front of the sports section highlighting my performance, barely acknowledging that Enloe had defeated Cary. Coach Williams called me over to the bench during practice. He told me to count how many times I used the word "I" in that article. It was a high number. I had referred to myself in a way disrespectful to my team. He wanted me to know it was about the team and not about me. He pointed that out using choice words. Man, he could curse.

On the basketball court, his mind-body-team approach worked.

At each practice, before we ever touched a basketball, we ran five miles. That's an exhausting pre-practice routine. If he gave us a break, it would be to run an endless number of steps or 125 laps around the gym. "This guy is crazy!" became a common expression among my teammates. We complained, of course, out of earshot. Mostly we did what we were told, because extensive running got us into incredible shape. Our legs were stronger than we could have ever imagined.

"The harder you work," Coach would say, "the tougher it is for you to surrender."

Coach Williams ran every mile with us. He matched us step-for-step when we climbed the bleacher stairs. During our five-mile runs, he finished near the front. He matched our push-ups and lifted heavier weights than we did.

"I made sure that when we came up against an opponent, he wasn't going to beat us because we were out of shape," he told me. "My job as coach is to make sure I know the X's and O's and have you prepared physically."

He told us if there were a team equal in skill, they surely were not as fit.

"You had to be in tip-top shape," Williams said. "And if you're tired in the fourth quarter and you look at your opponent, if he's tired, you think about those pre-practices."

Coach Williams said by exercising with us he was able to endear himself to the team and earn trust. "I had to convince you, first of all, by being part of what you were doing," he said. "So you accepted me because I was part of what you were doing."

For Frank Williams, no detail was too small. Tuck your shirt in, he would tell us. Pull your pants up. Brush your hair. Extend your arms on two-handed passes. Too often for my taste, his directives were directed at me. After a poor showing during one Friday game, Coach required a Saturday practice. No one wanted to be there, and the team sulked and played tired. That day, he called my name for every violation he could find. He pushed me to my breaking point. We held an intra-squad scrimmage and the other side set up in a 2-3 zone. I was waiting to help our point guard at the far end of the court. He took the ball out of bounds and threw it to me in bounds. I tapped the ball with my fist back to him. Coach Williams exploded, barking my name again.

He said the pass was unorthodox and screamed at me to use my fundamentals the way he taught. He wanted me to put two hands on the ball and make a traditional chest pass. He despised street basketball and loose fundamentals. Finally, he instructed me to "get the hell out of the practice." I was tired of him riding me. I lost my cool. I took my jersey off and threw it on the court. I quit the team. I walked to the locker room and slammed the door, cursing along the way.

Coach Williams burst through the locker room door as if he had snatched it off the hinges. Scared me half to death. He came at me, shouting about what I had done. Tears raced down my cheeks. "What in the hell do you think you're crying for?"

Then he sat on a bench. I explained my side of the story, how I felt abused and unnecessarily called upon. He cut me off. "You think you've been through something?"

He revealed that he had traveled a similar road.

Frank Williams grew up in Walnut Terrace, a depressed area in Raleigh near Shaw University, where he was born in 1953, the fourth of eight children. His father was an alcoholic whose difficulty handling that disease fractured the family. Eventually his father left the house. His mother, Queen Esther Williams, became a single parent. With his father out of work and not paying bills, the family struggled with limited income and that led Williams, at a young age, to take odd jobs. "I wanted out so badly," he said.

He cut grass, fixed bicycles and delivered goods to avoid going home to an empty dinner table. Because of this responsibility he grew up quickly and solidified the ideal family in his mind. "I knew what I wanted for my family at an early age," he said. "And I knew it took a good woman, so a woman similar to my mother." His mother was resourceful, preparing meals for the community – chicken and fish plates – that she sold out of their house on weekends.

As I listened, I began to see the similarities we shared. We both overcame hardships when we were young and were exposed to poverty and the emotional strife that comes with hungry nights. We had to work to purchase our basketball shoes. He told me about paying $6 for a pair of Chuck Taylor basketball shoes when he got to high school. Everyone around him, it seemed, was poor and discontented. "There were so many factors as a black kid growing up," he said. He recalled the riots that befell Raleigh after the assassination of Dr. Martin Luther King Jr. in April 1968.

He was 14 when rioters set Raleigh ablaze. He watched as people threw rocks out of anger and ran through the streets, smashing storefront glass and setting fire to buildings. The National Guard surrounded his neighborhood to control the riots.

The rioters' anger was visceral, he said. He understood their rage. He felt a sense of displacement and tried to understand "racism" and "inequality," words batted around like baseballs. "I was stereotyped as to not be anything," he said. "Never going to be anything because I was black and I was a black man."

Williams leaned on his teachers and coaches at Ligon, an all-black high school in Raleigh. They were proud people who believed an education could change a young man's life. He showed perseverance and passion that convinced teachers and coaches to help him get to college. With the projects at his back, the drug addicts and alcoholics buried in his past, he separated himself from his environment and achieved. In 1971, he received a basketball scholarship to Elizabeth City State University. He graduated with a major in industrial arts and technology.

"I needed coaches, I needed teachers that were instrumental," he told me. "Be smart enough to know that if you don't know something, [you should] surround yourself with people who can give you what you need." Coach Williams took courses in education to become a teacher and a coach. "I wanted to give back," he said.

Listening to him closely on that locker room bench gave me a perspective many players never have in understanding their coach. He was like me in so many ways it surprised me. His approach suddenly made sense. His life had made him tough and his concern for us had made him a taskmaster. I couldn't quit after learning his story.

"If you give up now and you walk off this court, you're letting down all your teammates, you're letting down the coaches, you're letting down your teachers, you're going to let down your family," he said. "How are you going to acquire things in your life? How are your dreams going to come true?"

He said he would want to break my neck if I quit, and I believed him. His stonemason hands looked as if they could snap a neck. He told me he loved me and that no other coach would care for me quite like he did. I believed him.

"I wiped my face, regained my composure and went back out there and just prayed to the Lord that you would feel the same way," he told me. "I just prayed. And when we got out there on the court, you came back out there."

I apologized to the team. I became a leader that day.

INSIDE THE

LOCKER ROOM

I'm not sure who I would be as a person or a coach
without the influence of coach Frank Williams.
Everything he demanded of me as a player I demand
of my players – except for wearing skirts, because the
NCAA might have a rule against such punishment. I am
a 10.0 version of him, accounting for changes in society
over the past 20 years.

On game days, I expect my players to dress neatly in a
shirt, tie and slacks. At Enloe, we always boarded the bus
in a suit and tie on game days. Coach Williams demanded that our hair was combed and our faces groomed. His
rules reigned supreme and I absorbed them. I've adjusted
a little to the times, but I haven't turned the team over to
my players. After a loss, the bus ride home is still silent.
What is there to talk about? Playing time is not an issue
discussed with players or parents. Playing time is earned
in practice. I stress this every season.

Parents were spectators during our time with Coach
Williams. They were not assistant coaches sent to save
their children from discipline. We were shown the way of
the world: Coach is going to set you straight, no matter

what you think, and no one could do anything about it. Basketball is a microcosm of life. Someone is going to press your buttons and demand accountability from you.

During press conferences, I almost always deflect personal attention in favor of talking about the team. I'm not the one taking shots, running around screens or playing defense. It's always about the team. There's a satisfaction in considering others. I learned that under Coach Williams. And when I defer to friends and family in other aspects of my life, I'm rewarded with the same feeling of satisfaction.

We won three conference championships under Coach Williams' guidance. He taught us the fundamentals of basketball. With the help of my teammates, I became conference player of the year as a senior and led the team in scoring. More important, though, I learned the fundamentals of life.

You can't run and quit, no matter who's in your feelings. Coach Williams taught me to be a man. That's what coaching is about for me – trying to build young men. They are our future leaders. They are future husbands. They are future fathers. (Just as women are our future leaders, wives and mothers.) I'm committed to coaching and teaching, rather than enabling.

I've seen the impact of enabling. One Christmas holiday, I went to Wal-Mart to do some last-minute shopping. There was a child begging his mother for a toy. At first the mother's response was an emphatic "no." The child kept begging and begging and begging and begging. Then he started to whine. The mother peppered him with "no," trying to ignore his pleas. Over time, however, her "no" grew softer and softer. Then faint. When they left the aisle, the child held his toy and five others.

This child was no different from any child. He acted as children do, pushing to see how far he could go. His mother failed.

This child learned that if he pouts, cries and begs, he'll get his way. His mother rewarded negative behavior. Now this child may grow up and expect everyone to bend to his whims and demands. God forbid he becomes a basketball player who doesn't know how to navigate adversity and pouts to get his way. If he is accustomed to getting his way and the calls don't go his way, then he'll pout on national TV, just like his mother taught him.

It seems Big Mamas like mine have faded like dinosaurs.

With my mother, there was one way: her way. She wasn't worried about being my friend. We were never friends. When my mother walked me into a store, she held out my hand and said, "You better not pick up nothing or ask for nothing." Under those rules, if I asked for something, she'd hit me; in turn, knocking me out right in the store. She showed off right in the aisle. There was no compromising.

The lesson carries over to building young men. There's no pouting as an adult. There's no pouting as a father with a family. I ask my players to think about being a family man with a wife and child. Then I tell them to think about working for a boss who asks you to complete an assignment that's out of your comfort zone. Do you pout? Do you take your stress home to your family? Or do you hold it down? Do you rise to the challenge and handle the work situation? Do you walk through the maze of life and find a way for your family?

As I think back, recalling the days when our legs cramped from running, remembering the coach who saved my life, I know that somebody prayed for me.

CHALKBOARD

1. What's your Decision?: We all reach a breaking point in our lifetimes. Normally, it occurs when we are angry or frustrated. At that moment, we may not realize that the five seconds beyond that breaking point are critical. Your decision – how you react in that moment – will affect the rest of your life. It's important to take time and think through the situation. I failed to give myself thinking time and my emotions got the best of me, which could have cost me my future. I was one step from becoming a has-been. High school coaches held the power in those days and Coach Williams could have kicked me off the team and discouraged college coaches from recruiting me. I am so glad he found it in his heart to give me a second chance. If not, there's no telling where my life would be.

2. Don't Mistake Teaching and Coaching for Criticism: Nowadays so many students/players/people are unable to accept teaching and coaching. Everything is fine as long as you're stroking their egos, or telling them what they would like to hear. But they rebel when challenged by someone with hopes of making them better. They get in their feelings and miss the value of the lesson. A teacher or coach can see things in their students and players they can't see in themselves. Their job as leaders is to squeeze the juice out of the orange to propel you to the next level. If not, they are allowing you to slide by and, in the long run, failing to teach you.

When confronted with this challenge, do not mistake coaching for criticism. You will have missed the point. Embrace the teachers' or coaches' challenge because they are trying to make you better.

3. Push Yourself: If there is anything I learned from Coach Williams, it's that the human body can do things you didn't think possible. I never knew how long I could run without stopping until I was introduced to pre-practice. We ran five continuous miles every day. That's before we ever dribbled a basketball. A man has a breaking point, and it is usually far beyond what his mind tells him initially. Your breathing comes under control, your legs feel stronger and your energy levels increase. Sure, it takes concentration and dedication, but when you dig deep and push yourself beyond, the rewards are so great.

CHAPTER 11

GOING TO MEET JAY-Z
(AS TOLD BY 9TH WONDER)

*"In the field of observation, chance
favors the prepared mind."*
Louis Pasteur, French biologist, born 1822

*I attended N.C. Central University from 1992-96. I met Pat Douthit, a.k.a
9th Wonder, in a history class called "The Black Experience Since 1865." He
sat close to the front, while I sat in the back. He answered questions with a
seriousness that stood out, yet his quiet demeanor seemed to blend into the
crowd. He was definitely prepared for class. Music, though, was his passion.
Wherever you saw him around campus, he was wearing earphones. As we
became friends, it became clear that he was special. The world soon took
notice, his musical talents spilling out of radios from Raleigh to New York
City. I invite you to be inspired by his story.*

– LeVelle Moton

C hance favors the well-prepared. It's a mantra I live by and one that perfectly describes my rise as a hip-hop producer. In all that I do, I believe in a methodical approach built on readiness, a sense that before I've arrived I have done everything within my power to meet the majesty of the moment. No matter the situation, as daunting and unimaginable as one's imagination can create, I am comfortable because my training, sharp as a Jedi Knight, started years in advance. My responsibility, in whatever room, is to remember what I've been taught and to execute.

It didn't matter that it was Young Guru on the phone asking me if I would come play some of my beats for Jay-Z. It didn't matter that they wanted me to fly from North Carolina to New York and meet them at Baseline Studios. It didn't matter that I – an underground producer with a modicum of success at the time – was invited to audition before one of the greatest rappers of all time, who in 2003 was making what he called "The Black Album," supposedly his last. It didn't matter that I was selling beats mail order for $100. None of that mattered.

I was prepared.

My birth name is Pat Douthit. I go by the stage name of 9th Wonder. I've produced music for some of the world's most acclaimed artists, including Mary J. Blige, Destiny's Child, Erykah Badu, Kendrick Lamar, Drake, Chris Brown, Ludacris and many more. I am a proud member of the Zulu Nation, founded in the early 1970s by Afrika Bambaataa. I was born in Winston-Salem, N.C., on January 15, 1975. I found hip-hop on 1086 East 17th Street in the Cleveland Avenue Homes where my uncle and aunt lived in Winston-Salem. It was 1982 and I was 7. Hip-hop became a part of me like a right arm or a left big toe. I learned about the music form, which was born in the Bronx, like I learned to play instruments – clarinet, saxophone, trombone, French horn, percussion. From elementary school through high school, I participated in band.

You could say I was a band geek. In general, I did very well in school and have always had a desire to learn history. I performed well in high school, taking honor courses. I come from a blue-collar family that expected me to pursue as many educational opportunities as possible. My mother was a teacher and my father was a self-made man who worked at R.J. Reynolds Tobacco as a landscaper. At 14, the summer before my freshman year in high school, I was accepted into a Wake Forest University program for minority students, where high achievement, academic success, self-determination and discipline were drilled into our minds. We problem-solved and read books like "The Isis Papers" and "The Conspiracy to Destroy Black Boys" by Jawanza Kunjufu. We developed a sense of pride and learned self-sufficiency, how we could compete, thrive and survive in any situation.

After graduation, in 1992, I enrolled at N.C. Central University, where history and music were my two favorite subjects. You rarely spotted me around campus without my headphones – and not any Beats By Dre. My set was duct taped to keep the wires from falling out. This was during the Golden Age of hip-hop, so I let my tape rock until my tape popped. We were blessed to have Biggie, Tupac, Redman and Nas on the radio at the same time. I loved it all. At first, I didn't know quite what I wanted to become professionally, but I knew it would evolve around my love for history and music. After four years of college, making it consistently on the Dean's List, I dropped out in 1996 to pursue my dreams of making beats as a DJ and producer. I started making beats in 1998 and have never stopped.

One never knows when it's their turn to shine. I certainly wasn't expecting a phone call from T. Smith, a photographer who had come to Raleigh to film a rapper named Spit Tank. His real name is Mervin Jenkins, and at the time he was a serious rapper who also was an assistant principal at Chapel Hill High in Orange County, N.C.

T. Smith chilled with us for an entire day before Spit Tank's show. He watched me work and I played him some music. He said, "If I ever hear anybody needs some beats, I'll make sure, you know what I mean, that, um, I'll hit you up." He was a cool dude, but I didn't think anything of what he said.

At that time my soon-to-be wife was working but I wasn't. I was selling beats through the mail. I had sold three to this guy from Portland for $750. This was before the Internet was poppin' and changed the way business was conducted around the world.

Months passed and I was still making beats. I remixed Nas's album "God's Son," calling it "God's Stepson – Nas." Then my brothers and I, Phonte and Big Pooh, dropped our first album, *The Listening*, as the rap trio Little Brother, in February 2003. I met both of those guys at N.C. Central where I was a student. As a group, we were casting our net and trying to find where we belonged in the music/hip-hop industry. We believed in our sound and knew it was original and different from what was out there. It was only a matter of time.

June arrived with heat, as it always does in North Carolina. The month also brought my first major beat sale. Master Ace of the Juice Crew in New York had heard my music and complimented the sound. He came to Raleigh to play the Lincoln Theater and I gave him a beat CD. From that, he released a song called "Good Old Love." I received $2,000 for that beat and that was a lot of money to me. Selling music to an established artist like Master Ace encouraged me more than ever to keep producing music.

Later that month, I saw an advertisement in a magazine for "The Black Album" that listed producers Jay-Z had worked with before: Dr. Dre, Kanye West, D.J. Premier, D.J. Quick, Timbaland. I thought, "Dang that might be a great album," even though I wasn't really feeling his music at the time. As an underground artist, I felt Jay-Z's content wasn't complex. Still, as I was maturing, I was learning objectivity and appreciation. Although I wasn't a fan, I couldn't deny his greatness, but it took me a while to fully grow into that concept. Jay-Z could rhyme and that was at the core of hip-hop. After some serious contemplation, I made up my mind that if he wasn't the best MC in 2003, I didn't know who deserved that title.

The Listening had taken off and opened space for a place on tour with the Hieroglyphics. I didn't want to go on tour. I wanted to stay home and make beats. Our manager at the time, I'll never forget this, said, "The only way you'll do that is if somebody like Jay-Z calls you."

Talk about speaking things into existence. He made that statement in August. On Sept. 17, 2003, I was returning home from the grocery store as Hurricane Isabel was threatening the region. I walked into the house and my phone rang. T. Smith said, "Yo man, what's going on?" I didn't know who he was. He said, "This T. Smith, you know, I filmed 'Spit Tank.'" That jarred my memory.

"What up, dog? What's going on? I haven't talked to you in six, seven months. What's up?"

He said, "I got somebody here who wanna talk to you man, about you playing some beats for Jay-Z."

I said, "You must be crazy."

He laughed, "I'm serious, man."

T. Smith put Young Guru on the phone. I had never met him, but knew he was Jay-Z's senior engineer and confidant. He starts off praising Little Brother, and expressed how much he enjoyed the music as a fan. I was honored and humbled.

"Wow, this is nuts," I said, thinking about how far I had come from enjoying hip-hop music as a child. I was living in my home state, which is so far removed from the entertainment industry, and light years removed from New York, the birthplace of hip-hop. I felt like I was encased in a bubble; sometimes I didn't know what was going on. These things run North Carolina: Jesus, tobacco, NASCAR and ACC basketball. You pick the order.

"How did you hear about Little Brother?" I asked Young Guru.

"I bought it at Fat Beats," he said, "and I played it, you know, we played it around the studio. You know who listened to it? Just Blaze listened to it. Kanye listened to it."

I couldn't believe it.

"Yeah, man, we talk about it all the time," he said. "Why don't you see if you can come up here and play beats for Jay?"

So that was it. With that invite, my travel plans had been decided. I called my wife into the room. "Do you know who that was on the phone?"

"Ah-no," she said.

I played back the entire conversation. We looked at each other as if Hurricane Isabel had plunged through our roof. That was a surreal moment for us, considering we had just been married on July 22, 2003. Our lives were changing in ways we had not discussed or expected.

Not one for excessive celebration, I headed straight to the computer. While I had 13 new beats in my system, I thought, "I don't have enough." I needed some fire. From that Wednesday until I left on Saturday, I made 30 beats in anticipation of my audition. In all, I had made 1,198 beats before I went to meet Jay-Z. I had sold only about six of them before getting to New York.

We arrived in New York and I called Ahmir "Questlove" Thompson, famous drummer for The Roots. He put my wife and I on a train to Philadelphia because the studio session was later that night. We hung with The Roots before heading back to New York. Questlove, who is friends with Jay-Z, had also called him on my behalf. I was grateful because the order of my life had moved at warp speed in a matter of months. From mail orders to Master Ace to meeting the most successful hip-hop artist of my generation. And then I was walking into the chaotic vibes of New York's Manhattan, lights blaring and traffic bustling and people busy with life.

Breathe the city in and it's intoxicating. Fortunately, though, I handled the atmosphere and never stumbled. At 28, I was grounded. My immature days were behind me and I focused on the task before me. We arrived at the hotel and I called a friend, a member of the producer crew, JUSTUS League. He came through with his girlfriend who took my wife to the movies to watch, ironically, "The Fighting Temptations," starring Beyoncé. We caught a cab to Baseline Studios, between 26th and 27th streets.

Jay-Z's bodyguard, Samson, a 6-foot-9 Samoan, greeted us at the front door of the studio. We took seats in the pool table room. On the wall, there was a framed jersey of Malik Sealy, a former basketball star at St. John's who died in a car accident. He was a friend of Jay-Z's. Young Guru came down the hall and he was taller than me at 6-foot-3. It was my first time meeting him and we dapped. "Come on back," he said.

We walked back to Studio A and Jay-Z was sitting on a middle console before a large track board.

He turned and looked at me and said, "So wassup, man?" He continued, "You come highly recommended by Ahmir, Questlove, see."

"I just want to thank you for the opportunity ... An opportunity of a lifetime."

Beyoncé, his girlfriend at the time, was lying on the couch behind us. I didn't know that for certain at the time. I thought it might have been her but I wasn't there reporting for TMZ. I was taught to handle my business before any socializing. "So what you got?" Jay-Z said.

I played him two beats and he remained poker faced. I played him a third and he made this face, like a ghoul, like What in the hell? That was a face of approval. I proceeded to play 26 more beats. The songs he liked, he looked down at the CD counter to see what number was playing. He named 3, 6, 9, 15 and so forth, for the tracks he liked. I played those for him again.

Jay-Z took the CD out and asked, "Where you from, man?"

"Winston-Salem."

"What's your story?"

"Man, I was in band in sixth grade," I said, going on to explain a little of my background. I expressed how much I love all music.

I may have explained that I had dropped out of college to pursue a career as a D.J. and a producer. The hardest part was telling my mother I didn't want to finish school with only a couple of semesters left. I left N.C. Central and took odd jobs, even one working at a Planet Smoothie. Times were hard in 2001. I used to trade drinks for food next door at Bruegger's Bagels. Most importantly, though, I let Jay-Z know that music ran in my blood, and I was certainly familiar with his contribution to the game.

"I'm not saying this 'cause I'm sitting here, I think you are probably the best MC walking right now," I said.

"Man, I gotta find a way to figure all this out," he said. "What you doin' on Monday?"

"What do I need to do be doin' on Monday?"

"You be back here."

"Okay."

Jay-Z left the room. Thirty seconds later he returned and asked, "Can I have that beat CD to ride to?"

"Hell yeah, you can have it," I said.

That was an intense night. I left the studio around midnight and walked about 20 blocks on a natural high. I was just walking and calling everyone I knew who could handle such sensitive information. Eventually we ended up in Times Square, where I met my wife. That was Saturday, Sept. 20, 2003.

Two days later I was back at Baseline Studios. I arrived a half-hour early for our 3:30 p.m. meeting. By that time, one of my good friends, Michael Burvick, had driven from North Carolina to support me in the studio. We met in college and he was the first person who listened to my beats regularly, and I thought he should be there for this occasion. As soon as he found out, he hit the road.

Jay-Z walked in the studio and said, "Play me some more shit." So I played him more. I had come with four CDs filled with music, plus a computer hard drive with more music stored.

"You got a lot of beats," he said. "I got this beat, and I got this song called 'Threat.' I want to see if you can make a beat of this sample."

He reached up on a speaker, grabbed a CD and handed it to me. "I'm gonna go get something to eat, be back." He left me there.

Earlier I had made a phone call to a friend of mine, Brainchild, who worked at Def Jam and asked him to bring me a new copy of Fruity Loops, a music software program. My version, for some reason, had failed. I loaded the new software onto a new IBM Thinkpad I bought from a friend for $700.

That PC only worked once. And it's on that machine that I made the track for Jay-Z. He didn't tell me how long he would take for lunch. I didn't know if he was getting takeout or sitting down at a fancy restaurant. So I went to work. He had given me a CD of R. Kelly's "A Woman's Threat" that he wanted me to sample from and create a track. I was definitely placed on the spot, in what could have been a make-or-break situation, but I felt comfortable chopping the sample and adding it over a New York bounce beat I structured.

I made the beat in about 20 minutes.

Later, D.J. Clark Kent had joined the room, along with Just Blaze. Rapper Freeway bounced in and out. Young Guru was in the front room shooting pool with Beyoncé and Cedric the Entertainer. Jay-Z had returned. "What you got?" he asked. I plugged the headphones into the computer and he listened.

"Yeah, that's what I need from you," he said.

I tracked the beat out and gave the completed version to Young Guru to place on the master track board. They turned the beat up ear-piercingly loud. "Man, this is nuts," I said. With the whirlwind storming around me, it seemed like I was dreaming in Technicolor.

Jay-Z went into the recording booth. I took a seat in one of the chairs facing the master track console. He turned down the lights in the booth. All you could see were hands and a gold watch. He started with ad libs: "I done told you [expletive]/ The 9 on me, stop [expletive] with me/ You [expletives] must got nine lives/ 9th Wonder." Once he said my name, it was over.

I understood Jay-Z's popularity at the time. He was probably the only rapper who could make a producer famous. It was widely accepted that a producer can make a rapper famous, but the reverse rarely happened. So I understood the magnitude of the moment, when my name was etched in history by Jay-Z calling it out on the track, "Threat."

He did the first verse in one take and came out and said, "What'd you think?" Of course, I agreed it was hot. It was hard to be critical, considering the position I sat in. He said he wanted me to produce the track. It was an honor. After Jay-Z left the room, Young Guru said, "Start shopping for a house."

In between verses, Jay-Z played Madden NFL video game with my friend Michael Burvick. Whipped him. There was also a Monday Night Football game blaring on the television, commanding everyone's attention. Yet he was focused. He wrote his second verse standing against the back wall. No pen or paper. He stood there and wrestled with the words inside his mind and created the verse from scratch. Unreal. Pure hip-hop.

He did the second verse in one take.

"The Black Album" was released on Roc-A-Fella Records on November 20, 2003. My track made the album as song No. 7, "Threat." It comes after "Dirt Off Your Shoulder," produced by Timbaland, and before "Moment of Clarity," produced by Eminem and Luis Resto. Other producers on that album were: Kanye West,

D.J. Quik, Just Blaze, The Buchanans, Aqua and 3H and The Neptunes. Incredible.

My work on "The Black Album" opened doors. I received $10,000 for "Threat," after previously receiving $300 for my work. Shortly after I returned home, Jay-Z called and asked for me to go to Los Angeles to work on Destiny's Child album, "Destiny Fulfilled," which was released November 2004. I produced three tracks on that album and worked with the group in the studio to create the music.

Next thing I know, I'm working with artists across the industry. Jay-Z mentioned me to Mary J. Blige and that's all it took. Soon her record company called me with instructions on how to submit music for her album, "The Breakthrough." That record, released in December 2005, won eight Grammy Awards, and for my contribution, a song titled, "Good Woman Down," I received that prestigious award. Amazing.

My phone continues to ring. I am grateful to Jay-Z for the opportunity to audition for "The Black Album." I am equally thankful to my parents, teachers and mentors, who helped prepare me for a chance meeting that changed my life. There was no Plan B. Preparation was essential in handling such a pressure-filled moment. Without it, I would have been, as they say, lost at sea.

INSIDE THE

LOCKER ROOM

Since I spent two days in the studio with Jay-Z, my life has changed in ways my wife and I never dreamed. My personal economy has grown. Young Guru was right when he said, "Start shopping for a house." It wasn't long before we purchased a home. I have traveled the world and shared musical experiences with talented people of all nationalities, faiths and creeds. I've built a hobby into a vocation into a thriving business. Instead of crafting beats in my friend's apartment, a makeshift studio we nicknamed Missie Anne, I now work out of a studio in Raleigh.

So much has changed except for my mantra: Chance favors the well-prepared.

There are so many elements from my story about meeting Jay-Z that are transferrable to other genres, whether it's politics or sports. Preparation is the underlying connection. Strong fundamentals enable one to face high-pressure, bend-or-break moments. Discipline, patience, repetition and respect are part of those fundamentals. And you start adding those characteristics into your arsenal at a young age, working on them as part of your everyday life, sculpting the muscle memory that will guide you in critical times. One should never underestimate the power of education or school where you stockpile these fundamentals.

Understand that problem-solving and decision-making skills are key elements of preparation. I credit my parents with teaching me basic fundamentals, forcing me to think critically about certain situations. Yet I was lucky to be chosen among Winston-Salem's young for the academic program at Wake Forest University before I started as a freshman in high school. There we took classes that bolstered my confidence and provided a guidebook no matter the situation. We learned to think critically about the world and to determine our place in the world. We emerged prepared to engage the powerful. We learned how to comport ourselves and recognize when certain decorum was necessary to achieve certain results.

For instance, when I walked into Baseline Studios, I wasn't there to fraternize with the guests, meaning there was no chatting with Beyoncé or playing pool with Cedric the Entertainer or questioning Jay-Z about his latest car. I was there on official business and I had to understand the moment and how to conduct myself. I was there to possibly change my life forever.

I was determined to not make a fool out of myself. I avoided telling jokes or sharing stories or soliciting information about other producers. I provided information as it was requested, carefully crafting the story I wanted my future employer to know about me. I was honest but terse.

Mentors such as Dr. Ernest Wade at Wake Forest exposed us to books such as "The Conspiracy to Destroy Black Boys" by Jawanza Kunjufu and poetry books by poets such as the late Maya Angelou, who was a distinguished professor at the university. I understood my worth and was prepared if the time came to meet seemingly larger-than-life figures. They were humans, too, who only needed to be treated with respect; revered for their accomplishments yet never feared or pampered. I allowed Jay-Z to guide the audition and met him firmly in the middle, demonstrating my skills more than my personality. I wanted him to like me, though I knew that could only come with extended time spent together. I was more concerned with showcasing my talents than being popular.

My biggest fear was getting an opportunity and fumbling in the spotlight. There wasn't a beam of light that could have distracted me from my task. I walked in Baseline Studios, a half-hour early, determined to represent myself to the fullest. If it were basketball, I had practiced my best moves, shot my free throws and planned to score 30 points, grab 10 rebounds and make 10 assists. A triple-double was in my future.

A buzzer-beater was possible. That was based on the 10,000 or more hours I had spent making beats on my own, building them from sounds in my mind to full tracks on the computer screen. Before I showed up, I had built beats with Fruity Loops and programs like it for years. I knew that program like I invented it. I wasn't there as an intern. I had learned, studied and mastered my craft.

When I sat down at my laptop inside Baseline Studios, there was no second-guessing myself. I knew exactly how to chop a sample and create a New York bounce beat underneath. Jay-Z, who made "The Black Album" in a month, had played for me many of the tracks that were completed. I understood the standard he was looking for, yet I wasn't intimidated by the task. Considering the circus around me, I cleared my mind and transported myself back to North Carolina where I made beats every day. It was normal for me to sit down and create from scratch. So it was no problem with the pressure-cooker turned on high.

I'd seen too many people get their moment and blow it. Perhaps they weren't ready for prime time, but most likely they just weren't prepared along the way. The fundamentals weren't coded into their DNA. Perhaps they were too fearful to give that big speech in elementary or middle school, or weren't interested in debate club where they could have practiced public speaking without a cost attached to how they performed. Perhaps they never asked for that solo in band or read for that lead acting role in theater. Maybe they never tried out for basketball, giving self-deprecating excuses as to why everyone was better than them.

Nothing fazed me when I went to work. Not the master track board at the fancy studio. Not the mega star Beyoncé sitting on the couch or the comedic genius Cedric the Entertainer playing pool. Instead of stargazing, I integrated him on the track. I was ready.

I was humble. I checked my ego at the hotel before catching a cab to the studio. There's nothing worse than a stranger boasting about himself and acting flamboy-ant to draw attention. I let others speak for me. I let my music speak for me.

Years later, I was blessed to speak to students about hip-hop music. My career in the classroom started at N.C. Central University, a familiar place that gave me a foundation with courses such as "The Black Experience Since 1865." Though I never graduated – a few credits short – I was asked to be an artist-in-resident at N.C. Central University in 2006. The breadth of my experi-ence there was eye-opening. I hosted seminars and workshops, while working in studio with students. I also developed a course call "Hip Hop in Context, 1973-

1997." I've always loved history and having the chance to delve into the important events and dates that traced a hip-hop timeline was exciting and rewarding. I enjoyed the students and I found my inner teacher.

Since 2004, I have been an adjunct professor at Duke University, where I co-teach classes such as "The History of Hip-Hop." In 2013, I was awarded the Nasir Jones Hip-Hop Fellow at Harvard University, where I was a lecturer in African American Studies, specifically topics related to hip-hop music. I was a three-year resident at The Hip-Hop Archive, located in the W.E.B Du Bois Institute in African and African American Studies department. One of my lectures, entitled "These are The Breaks," was based on the history and culture of hip-hop, but was also connected to my relationship to the music as a producer. Dr. Henry Louis Gates, the Alphonse Fletcher University Professor at Harvard University, and Dr. Marcyliena Morgan, the director of the archive, encouraged me to share my knowledge as an expert on the subject of hip-hop after 20 years in the business. I taught a class called the "The Standards of Hip." As part of my residency, I also researched, which lead to a project where I ranked the top 200 hip-hop albums of all time.

Society doesn't often group black genius and hip-hop together. Yet those two phrases come together to describe what has taken shape over the course of 30 years. Urban youth, primarily blacks and Puerto Ricans in New York, cultivated a culture around DJing, breakdancing, MCing and graffiti arts. That culture bled into American society, leaked into international waters and became a global phenomenon. I am part of the first wave of scholars who have examined the music, explored its many layers and set out to academically define its composition.

As higher education goes, Harvard sets the standard. So to name the top 200 hip-hop albums of all time is an honor and duty. These records will be catalogued at The Hip-Hop Archive and available at the Harvard University Library. Our work, other scholars and myself, is setting the standard for the future. When you ask a student to name a famous early 20th century artist, names like Picasso and Van Gogh, come up immediately. Somebody made that so. As an authentic voice in hip-hop culture, it's my job to point out the artists to be remembered, to say, "These are the classic artists you should study and here's why."

It's been an interesting journey since sitting in the studio with Jay-Z. I never thought it would lead to a fellowship at Harvard University.

I left home for college in 1992. Expectations were as tall as a Dubai skyscraper. With my track record in high school, having taken honors courses and made National Honor Society, I was the one the family counted on to make it big. I was the chosen one: The only Douthit who would finish college. My older brother played basketball and was ranked fourth in the state in 1982. His grades, however, weren't acceptable and he ended up at a community college. He left community college to play at Brandon University in Brandon, Manitoba, Canada for a few seasons. He chose the wrong crowd and became addicted to crack. He was 20. He fell into that alternative world hard, started dealing drugs, ending up in jail in 1997. He's been drug-free since 1996 and now works as a supervisor in Winston-Salem. My father was a proud landscaper. His father dug wells. My uncle was a kingpin.

My uncle died at age 40 in prison. He was incarcerated for dealing drugs in Winston-Salem. He was ruthless and destroyed many people's lives, including his own children's. Four of six children went to jail for selling drugs. His wife went to jail, too. My father's baby brother ran the Cleveland Avenue Homes and built a negative reputation that lives on today. His baby sister was a custodian, the only one of the siblings, aside from my father, to follow a straight path. This is my lineage.

So when I came home and told my mother I wanted to drop out, you can bet she wasn't happy. I don't suggest for anyone to take my path. Stay in school. My mother, I'm sure, wanted to grab me by the shirt and drag me back to campus. She wanted to know how she had failed me. She was a teacher for 44 years.

I assured her I would land on my feet or go back to school. Sure enough, I received the opportunity to teach at N.C. Central, bringing my experience full circle. My mother had no reason to worry because she was the one who believed in education and instilled in me the fundamentals that carried me through many doors. Without a college degree, I am the most successful Douthit in my family tree.

Bet your life on it: Chance favors the well prepared.

CHALKBOARD

1. Study Your Craft: After you discover what you're good at, study your craft to find success. "One must practice," is an obvious statement often overlooked. If you want your talents to grow, then you must invest long hours into developing them. But also study the history of your activity. Know more about what you're doing than anyone else. This lets others know you're serious. I made a commitment to hip-hop and I learned its history and culture. I studied producers and DJs who came before me and developed my style.

Before I ever visited with Jay-Z, I had made more than 1,000 beats. I made beats every day. I had mastered producer software such as Fruity Loops and Reason. I learned how to sample from old-school records, extract a drumbeat and use a synthesizer while assembling my beats. This all took time to master and I didn't stop tinkering with the programs until they were committed to muscle memory. Even after I mastered one thing, I still read magazines and books to bolster my technique. I treated my development like a history class and I learned about everything and everyone that had come before me. No one could surprise me with information about my craft because I had invested the time to learn the traditional and obscure. I became an expert in hip-hop.

When I speak to basketball players, I always ask them about their favorite players. Listening to their answers, I immediately know who has studied the game and who may have just watched current games on television. If you're going to be the best at your position, you should know who has already mastered that position before you. If you are a point guard, you should know the top 100 point guards to play the game. Learn from their history. It's the same with any field.

Survey yourself: How many hours do you spend with your current activity? How much money have you invested in upgrading equipment or advanced courses? How often do you consult others who have the same interest? How many books have you read about the subject? How many examples have you sought outside of your own?

2. Be Prepared: I didn't bat an eyelid when Jay-Z left me in the room with a limited time to turn around a beat for him and said, "I hope you have something when I come back." I didn't know what "a little while" meant, but I approached the task like another workday and found my comfort zone. I didn't feel the pressure because I was prepared.

I had spent sleepless nights flipping samples and I was ready when Jay-Z unexpectedly handed me R. Kelly's CD. I had prepared 1,300 beats on my computer for him to listen to but he had other ideas. He wanted me to create a beat from scratch and so I strapped on my headphones and went to work on my laptop. I didn't experience any computer problems because I had already updated my software and double-checked my hardware before I came through the door. I wasn't going down based on a technical error. I didn't know I would need my laptop but just in case I had it on hand. I chopped up that beat in 20 minutes.

3. Build Relationships: Respect everybody you meet. Every time I meet someone I introduce myself by name. I don't assume people know who I am. You never know when your interaction with a stranger may result into a beautiful business relationship or friendship. You never know who you're going to meet.

I was attending a D.J. conference in Phoenix, Ariz., and I wanted to go to a restaurant outside of the hotel. But it was summertime and the thermometer showed the temperature was more than 100 degrees. So I settled for lunch at the hotel bar. I remember looking at the TV and coverage of Chuck Daly, who had died, dominated the news. I sat beside a guy, who knew me. Still, I introduced myself, instead of acting like a big shot and thinking I was more important than anybody else.

He said, "I'm a fan." I thanked him. He complimented my shoes, a new pair of Cement 3 Nike Air Jordans. I like the brand and had splurged at a Flight Club shoe store in New York on a fresh pair. This guy continues to tell me how much of a fan he is of my music, naming albums and songs and going on and on. Some might have distanced themselves and called him a "stan." I thanked him profusely, genuinely appreciating the love. I asked his name.

"My name is Jason," he said. "You were here last year and you helped my brother. He makes beats."

"Yeah, I know the young dude," I said.

"You talked to him for about an hour," he said.

"You make beats?" I asked.

"No, that's my brother, I'm just here supporting him," he said.

"You like Jordans?" I asked. "I know someone if you're looking."

"No, I'm good," he said.

"What do you do," I asked.

"I just designed Jordan No. 23," he said.

When I met Jason Mayden, he was the creative director for Jump Man, which promotes Michael Jordan merchandise, including its Jordan brand of basketball shoes. He pulled out his black card with iconic logo of Michael Jordan jumping and told me to email him.

"I'll get you out of Flight Club jail," he said.

I didn't think much of it. I got home and I had three boxes sitting on my porch. You never know who you're going to meet. Respect everyone.

AFTERWORD

by

Mike Tomlin

Head Coach, Pittsburgh Steelers

am honored to be included in this important work. Coach Moton and I are what I refer to as, "coaching brothers." We share some common core beliefs: we are fundamentalist, we are teachers, we coach hustle and, most importantly, we believe you must develop personal relationships with those you coach.

But it goes beyond philosophy. We have a love affair with the games that have shaped our lives, as you can clearly tell from reading "The Worst Times Are the Best Times." These games – football and basketball – have helped lift us from poverty and tough environments. These games have provided the inspiration to live the disciplined lives that success requires. These games have motivated us to teach in hopes that the next generation can find refuge in their endeavors – the way we did.

Velle and I met several years ago in Latrobe, Pa., at a Steelers' camp. I often invite coaches to attend camp for a few days. I especially enjoy working with basketball coaches. There is always a great exchange of perspective. They are always interested in the regiment in football training, whereas football coaches are always interested in the intimacy in basketball training. I was instantly drawn to Velle because he is unguarded and upfront about his desire to get better as a coach, qualities that have served him well from what we've read in this book.

Those are two personal qualities I try to continually achieve. I can also relate to his desire to get better and learn from other professionals. You would be surprised how often I meet coaches who have all the answers. Velle and I quickly became friends. Our conversations tend to be about work and how we can grow together to improve at our craft. We talk about how we can become better men and better leaders for our teams, communities and causes.

As we continue our journey through life we are obligated to help others. Velle made that very clear in his stories and that was a critical message I hope everyone received. To have success and grow, one must consider others as part of the process. This is just one of the many lessons found in this book, which I found filled to capacity with wisdom. Velle's words sparked a flame and I commend his efforts.

We must continue to tell our stories to hopefully inspire the next generation to have the courage to chase their dreams. That's truly why this book is so important. It's our job to provide a blueprint for the next generation. In every story you can feel Velle's truth. He thought it was important to share the painful experiences about how he came up in order to help others establish their vision. We share the same sentiment when it comes to communicating our stories with young people. I learned so much more about him from these candid tales about his youth and will share these compelling stories with young people I meet.

Sports are awesome vehicles for young people to navigate the adversity that life throws our way. Whether it is Boston, Raleigh or Newport News young people need to know we love them. This book is an expression of that love – a spirited love letter that encourages readers to continue to fight for a better life. Use this book as a guide or as a conversation-starter. Velle's words convinced me once again that success is possible if you put God first, work smart and work hard.

— *Mike Tomlin*

Q&A WITH NEW EDITION'S RALPH TRESVANT AND MICHAEL BIVINS

by

Edward G. Robinson III

Interview with Ralph Tresvant, as told to Edward G. Robinson III

Q: In what way was LeVelle inspired by New Edition?

RALPH: He saw some people from the neighborhood, a group of guys who looked like him, the way he grew up. He walked around some of the same schools we went to. He really took from it – the positive things. Throughout the years, he was always very adamant about how much the clean-cut image of the group impacted him.

It helped him stay that way when it was easy to put your hat to the back and be where everybody was. But he stuck to his guns because he watched that work for us. I watched that: There was a big part of what he incorporated into his style and just his personality. He looked back later and said that was a big difference.

Q: What groups were you guys inspired by?

RALPH: There was some definite group imagery that we were looking at that said, "OK, we can do that." That was the Jacksons, Temptations and the Motown vibe. In our neighborhood they were doing Motown; it was heavy in the Orchard Park area we grew up in. I guess all the black areas at the time were full of that sound and the feel-good Smokey Robinson sound. What they were doing was influencing us to do the synchronized choreography, to transfer light and all that kind of stuff.

We were watching those guys. They stood out. What they did made you look like a group to us. We had people around the way who were with Maurice Starr. He had local groups he would put out that were pretty popular. The Untouchables. He had the Transitions. There were a couple groups he was managing around the way that we really looked at. And they would pull up in limos. We would just say, "Wow. Look at that." At a regular talent show, they would do this stuff.

We got a chance to see that kind of prestige. So there was local influence. Maurice Starr was in Boston doing talent shows and music. We wanted to join one of his talent shows. There were a lot of things in our neighborhood that we were able to look at, reflect and incorporate.

Q: What made you guys want to go so hard? Even from a young age you could see how hard you guys were dancing, and I know Brooke Payne had a lot to do with that.
RALPH: That was it. It was Brooke. He told us one thing one time in rehearsal and it stuck with every member. We were getting ready to perform in front of about 400 or 500 people and "Candy Girl" was out and was doing its thing. It was starting to fill up the charts. And I remember him saying, "It doesn't matter if you're in front of 500 or 5,000, you perform it the exact same way. You never know who is going to be in the audience watching you." We took that to heart and every time I hit the stage, I performed like a performance for the most important. This might be the important moment in my career. When you're on stage, you go hard, you know?

Q: What would you tell people about rehearsal or practice?
RALPH: It's the difference between being great and just being okay. We practice so hard, so much every day. Back in the day, we'd spend most of our hours after school in the Salvation Army Boys & Girls Club. We'd spend almost every day doing something that had to do

with being an entertainer or trying to get better at the craft that we were about to display in front of people, in front of the world.

It's not something you look at as work. You have to look at it as a part of what you do to get where you're going. You know, it's like if you want to learn how to drive a car, you've got to get in the car. You've got to do this every day until you get it right. So you want to do something until it becomes instinctive. It's just what you do. It's like when your shoe comes loose; you bend over and you tie it down. You don't think about how to do it anymore.

When we're watching others like Beyoncé, she's practiced, she's rehearsed. She's had that whip on her, on herself, and the people over her. From dad or whoever it might have been throughout the years. Just keeping her on it to the point where it became a part of her. She knows about imagery and the right clothes to wear. She knows a lot of things that go instinctively with becoming a great artist.

You learn those things. You practice those things. You practice being great. Every day. It's not something that you're working toward. You practice every day. I think that's how you have to see it to understand the final result. It's not like a goal per se. It's like if you're working out every day, you stay healthy. It's the same way with practicing and entertainment. If you do what you do all the time, you stay healthy at it. You get better.

Q: LeVelle studied your videos like game tapes and he learned every word and every step. Did you guys look at Michael Jackson like that? Did you study James Brown?
RALPH: Man, we studied with Travis Gresham, our first manager. He was sitting at the Salvation Army Boys & Girls club in the basement. We turned out the lights. We'd sit on the floor and he would cut off all the lights and play the Jacksons' live album from the beginning, with the crowd sounds. He wanted us to envision being

on stage, to envision what he was feeling. That was supposed to be us. The crowd was there. They were shouting to come out and they wanted to see us. It was that kind of a vibe.

Q: How often did you visualize?
RALPH: We did visuals at nine, 10, 11 years old. Yeah, we would sit down and envision being on stage, what it was like to be in their shoes and performing, and listen to the whole album in the dark. It used to begin and we'd do "Heartbreak Hotel." I remember that was a big part of what we wanted to be like or what it would be like to be in their shoes. It became natural. We expected to feel that feeling.

Q: Tell me what it was like to leave Orchard Park and have your family leave Orchard Park?
RALPH: That was more of the definition of making it. I didn't understand the charts. I didn't understand Billboard. I didn't understand that "Candy Girl" just knocked "Billie Jean" or "Beat It" down to the number two slot. It sounded good but it didn't make sense. As far as me measuring success, I didn't have any bearings. But [I understood] moving out of the projects, buying my mom a penthouse in Rolling Hills, California, her not having to clean at the Boys Club. She used to do maid service. She could retire from all that kind of stuff.

Q: Describe Orchard Park (public housing community, where you grew up.)
RALPH: It wasn't as bad when I was there, but it started to go there. It started to get to a point where it was really bad. A lot of killing. A lot of people dying, being shot. A lot of people being the victim of drugs, prostitution, extortion from all the people coming in from other areas. So I watched a lot of that stuff happen. And the climate changed a whole lot. I mean, it was always a place where you had to be tough.

Q: How did that impact people in the community?

RALPH: So all those projects bred a certain type of person, a type of environment that you had to hold your own. You couldn't be no punk. But it wasn't only about that. We still had a lot of community get-togethers. People still cared about each other. It wasn't all, you know, I'm going to get mine. It was a little different climate. So for us, we still had a little bit more family-oriented climate. It wasn't half bad as once we left and once we got out into the world. But I did know that it was the same in Chicago, Detroit, Los Angeles. All the way around the board, you know, was a reflection of what was happening in the black community. I got to see that as I was able to travel around and realized you weren't isolated, that it was happening in most of the places where we were.

Q: The subject came up about LeVelle dancing and holding his own with the group's steps. He feels like he's a member of the group. How would you rate his dancing and his keeping up with the steps with you guys?

RALPH: Thank God that LeVelle can coach.

Q: You don't think he can hold his own, man?

RALPH: Well, we'll have to see that. We'll have to one day put a coat on him while he's at one of these shows and he has to show his dance step. "Stop talking. Talk and walk the walk."

Q: Why are you so proud of LeVelle?

RALPH: This is huge to him. Huge to a brother coming out of Orchard Park the way we did. All of the accolades to him. I mean, I love just to talk about places that he's been. It's amazing to me. He's one of them kind of cats that hardly plugs himself. I think that he really deserves a book. This is amazing!

Interview with Michael Bivins, as told to Edward G. Robinson III

Q: There is a chapter in this book that describes how New Edition inspired LeVelle. Who inspired you guys?

MICHAEL: Coming up we were fans of all different type of artists, from Slade to the Jackson 5 to the Temptations. There were so many different things. It wasn't really so much about – when you are our age – getting into records. You just like whatever is being played on the radio, whatever they're playing at the block party. We liked Lakeside. You know, we liked Rick James before we even met him. So [New Edition] encompasses so many different styles and different artists and stuff from back in the 70s and the 80s. We were young like the Jacksons, so they assumed we were like the Jacksons, but we did routines like the Temptations. We were a little bit of everything.

Q: How does it make you feel to learn how inspired LeVelle was by your group?

MICHAEL: Every young kid wants to be like somebody who's on television, who's on the radio. So for him it was just like, Man, these young black kids are from the neighborhood! I see these kids, and it makes me want to do something as well. Some kids are bright enough to learn early what they want to be in life.

And some kids just enjoy their lives and they haven't really figured out what's that one thing they want to be, because they're still just being young. But sometimes when a young kid, eight or nine, is like, I'm gonna be a ball player. I'm gonna be a recording artist. And then you can see somebody else, and it helps you figure out how you want to be when you tap into who is as great as you are. Levelle was a basketball player and he got influenced more from sports, but he was also excited and happy for us because of what we were doing in music.

Q: Did you know the extent of how much he was watching you guys? I mean, he really kind of learned and took what you guys were doing to heart. That must be special for a group who tried to pour themselves out to their fans.

MICHAEL: I found out as he got older and we all were able to articulate what we were thinking then. Back then you just used the words "cool," "wow," you know, little simple words. But as you get older, you appreciate what we were doing at that age, the routines of The Temptations. What kids are driven to do those routines? What we were doing became so classic you could never look at it like it's gonna go out of style. We didn't have a traditional what's-hot-at-the-time style. We had a classic style from a classic group who were doing certain type of routines, which we call stepping.

That's what our man (choreographer) Brooke Payne called it. Stepping. We were already in a class by ourselves. So for a young kid who's got form and got style, he can appreciate our style because he knows other kids ain't really dancing like that. That's how our parents dance. They're stepping. So it all started then and it's about style, man. Style will always grab people's attention, but it's also the personality and the character that will keep people's attention.

Q: Is there anything you wanted to just share about LeVelle now?

MICHAEL: What was really special is the day he proposed to his wife. He did it at a New Edition concert. I thought that was his way of coming full circle in terms of "these are the kids that influenced me, childhood friends, and for me to marry this woman, what better platform to do it?" He just went with what his heart was, and his wife knowing him in basketball and New Edition stories. Even though he wasn't a performer on stage, he was on the stage with friends who made him feel like he was home. I thought it was unique and it's never happened before on our stage at a concert.

So he made history within the history that we've been making for 30 years. That's special and that's real because he chose to do it when we were there. It says a lot about how our roads continue to cross. He did say a lot about being from Boston and how Bostonians stick together, no matter what city we're in or where our travels take us. That's the one thing we got in common is we were just kids living a dream. We're still living our dreams.

Q: How does LeVelle fit into the group circle?
MICHAEL: I know he feels like he's in the group. So it's funny to me that when I'm talking, I got to talk to a guy that's not in the group who feels like he's in the group, and I think that's special in itself.

Q: You could take offense to that, but on the other hand, you find it special. Why is that meaningful?
MICHAEL: Because he's real, man. It's real. He can pick up the phone and call me. He can call Ralph. He knows everybody. It's real. It ain't no B.S., man.

Q: That makes it special?
MICHAEL: I walk around with a North Carolina Central University sweat suit compliments of LeVelle. And it's an honor to be a part of the family, for him to ask me to be a part of it, because it's not every day somebody calls your phone and wants to interview you because somebody is doing a book. You can't take calls like that for granted, man.

Q: Yeah. How would you rate his dancing with the routines?
MICHAEL: Man, I haven't seen him doing the slide in a minute, but I'm sure he's got that soul that he can't be too far off the beat. He knows what it is. If I would rate him, I would rate him high.

Q: He says he can step right in and take your place if you get an ankle twist. Is he ready?

MICHAEL: Oh man, I got to keep him away then. I might need to keep him on the injured reserve. That can't happen, man.

ACKNOWLEDGEMENTS

To every Kid I've coached from middle school to college: Thank you for the experience.

To every Coach that's ever coached me, Thank you for your time and patience. I know it wasn't easy.

To New Edition and Brooke Payne (Ronnie, Bobby, Ralph, Ricky, Mike, Johnny): You gave a boy from "humble beginnings" hope. It's because of you that I know Dreams come true. Thank you. Love you guys.

To my godmothers Maxine Wall & Connie Mitchell: I love you dearly. Thank you for believing in me.

To Ron Williams: Thank you for becoming the father I never had. The day I put a smile on your face is the day I knew I could conquer the world.

To everyone in the communities of Roxbury and Lane Street: I am who I am, and I am what I'm not, because of you. I love you guys.

To every teammate I ever had: Thanks for the brotherhood and memorable experiences.

To The Boys & Girls Club: You saved my life and taught me so much in return. Thank you.

To LuAnn Edmonds Harris: You are my second mother. Your heart is as good as gold. I love you.

To Cathy Moore & Celia Selden: You saw something in me that I didn't see in myself. You're not only my favorite teachers, but my favorite people of all time.

To every teacher that taught me: Thanks for your time, dedication and sacrifice.

To my spiritual mother Phyllis Jones: Your prayers and godly words keep me going. I love you mommy.

To my spiritual brother Pastor Nate Davis: Thank you for making me a better man, my brother.

Anyone that I didn't mention: Please charge it to my head and not my heart. I love you guys.

To my N.C. Central students, administration, fans & alums. Thank you for your undying support.

To my best friends in the world Shannon Godfrey & Taurus Davis: Your love is unconditional. your truth is valued, and your friendship is priceless. I love you

To my co-author Edward Robinson: Thank you for believing in me and making me look a lot better than I am. You brought out the best in me.   — *L.V.*

First, let me start by thanking LeVelle Moton for allowing me to take this journey with him. Much appreciated.

Thank you to all my teachers. Thank you to anyone who has ever read an article I've written. Thank you to any first time reader of my work. I appreciate your time. Keep reading. There's more to come.

Thank you to my family, mentors and friends, those souls who are here with me in the flesh and those souls who have gone on to grace. You taught me well.

A special thank you to my editor: Adrienne Johnson Martin, whose gifted hands sliced and diced without cutting too deep. Thank you to Natalie Stokes-Peters for sharing her publishing knowledge and helping to guide the ship. Thank you to Shawn Ashworth, who took on the job of preparing a resource guide without hesitation. Thank you to Antonio and Constance Teixeira, my loving uncle and aunt, who opened their home for me to complete this book.

And, finally, thank you to Andre Mays, whose generosity throughout this process made it possible.   — *E. G. R. III*

ABOUT THE AUTHOR

Edward G. Robinson III is an award-winning sports journalist who has written for *The Washington Post, The Pittsburgh Post-Gazette, The News & Observer* in Raleigh and other newspapers. A reporter for 15 years, he is a contributing writer for *The Washingtonian Magazine*.

Robinson covered ACC college football as a beat reporter for the Duke and Wake Forest teams and has written about high school football and basketball championships, collegiate bowl games, Final Fours, professional tennis tournaments, golf tournaments, and men's and women's lacrosse and soccer championships.

In 2014, he won The Society of Professional Journalists' Dateline Award for Excellence in Local Journalism for a story in *The Washingtonian Magazine*. He also has won awards from The Associated Press Sports Editors, The N.C. Press Association, *The News & Observer,* the National Association of Black Journalists and the Pittsburgh Black Media Federation. He was a finalist for the 2012-13 Nieman Foundation Fellowship at Harvard University.

Robinson earned a bachelor's degree in print journalism from American University in Washington, D.C., and a master's in non-fiction and fiction writing from Johns Hopkins University in

Baltimore, Md. A native of Washington, D.C., Robinson grew up playing tennis and watching countless hours of basketball. He lives in his hometown with his wife.

RESOURCE GUIDE

By Dr. Shawn Ashworth
Principal, Alternative Middle School
Arundel County Public Schools
Arundel County, Md.

Chapter 1 – Fatherless

1. What is the difference between a rent party in the 1970 and a house party of today?
2. What does the author mean by the statement, use my father's departure as a crutch?
3. How hard is it to avoid something you really want? Can you think of a time you avoided something or someone?
4. Why does growing up without both parents hurt? What are some positive lessons that you can learn?
5. After LeVelle Moton yearned for his father, why was he so angry when the letter came?
6. What does the author mean when he says; "he used my anger as fuel to motivate me?"
7. Write a letter. What advice would you give?

Vocabulary Words

1. notoriously	12. memorabilia	23. adversity
2. devoured	13. yearned	24. domestic
3. supplementing	14. self-hatred	25. heaping
4. crammed	15. proclaiming	26. prideful
5. scenario	16. relented	27. tortured
6. sugar-coating	17. confidence	28. dispirited
7. resentment	18. convinced	29. berserk
8. deserted	19. concoct	30. ferocity
9. callous	20. taboo	31. sulking
10. bolstered	21. disadvantage	32. exhaustion
11. camouflaged	22. ghetto	33. catastrophe

Chapter 2 – New Edition

1. Think about someone famous or someone you admire. Why/how have they changed your life?
2. Describe a time when you had to be persistent, dedicated or disciplined. What behaviors/characteristics did you demonstrate?
3. How do you use your internal voice to be disciplined, persistent and dedicated?
4. How can emulating someone's behavior be positive or have a positive impact on you?
5. What is the difference between looking up to someone and emulating someone's behavior?

Vocabulary Words

1. inspired
2. pursued
3. choreographer
4. progenitors
5. intricate
6. visionary
7. taskmaster
8. dignified
9. sequined
10. horrendous
11. devastating
12. symbolized
13. idolized
14. despised
15. elevated
16. emulated
17. invisible
18. synchronized
19. farcical
20. auxiliary
21. repertoire
22. competitive
23. medieval
24. dominated
25. diversification
26. quintets
27. hiatus
28. contemplating
29. advantageous
30. statistic
31. immersing
32. perfectionist

Chapter 3 – Strike Three

1. Why does the author refer to playing baseball as a love affair?
2. How can one person have the swag of so many people?
3. What did the author mean when he said, "He stuck the knife into a wound leaking?"
4. Why do you think LeVelle Moton kept reminding the reader that he was the youngest on the team? Does age impact your ability to be good/successful?

Vocabulary Words

1. grasping
2. captivated
3. nurtured
4. exploited
5. neophyte
6. ultimate
7. confidence
8. emulated
9. situational
10. euphoria
11. fundamentals
12. daunted
13. geyser
14. devastating

Chapter 4 – Guardian Angel

1. Why is important for LeVelle Moton to tell his grandmother that Marvin Gaye has died?
2. What's special about LeVelle Moton's relationship with his grandmother? Can you relate? If so, describe your relationship with your grandmother or grandfather?
3. Describe the way LeVelle Moton felt when his grandmother went to the hospital to fight cancer? Define cancer in your answer.
4. Why did LeVelle Moton consider his family's behavior dysfunctional?
5. What does LeVelle Moton mean by the phrase, "Power of prayer?"

Vocabulary Words

1. beloved
2. tragic
3. legacy
4. inquisitive
5. precious
6. divinity
7. exponentially
8. monumental
9. communication
10. dedicated
11. burglarized
12. dysfunctional
13. irreconcilable
14. arguments
15. interior designer
16. vibrancy
17. terminal
18. awe-inspiring
19. eulogy
20. adversity

Chapter 5 – Hot Shot

1. What sport can you play where what you wear has an impact on how you compete?
2. How did the trip change LeVelle Moton's life?
3. What did the author mean by the statement, "I delighted in the experience like it was my birthday?"
4. What does it mean to "compete with all your heart?"
5. What does support have to do with performing? Do people need support in order to be successful?

Vocabulary Words

1. pumped
2. guzzle
3. memorized
4. advantageous
5. reputation
6. anxious
7. simultaneously
8. exhilarating
9. underestimate
10. propelled
11. allotted
12. dividends
13. confident
14. curmudgeon
15. chided
16. cautious
17. chiseled
18. wracked
19. erupted
20. intrigued
21. exalting
22. euphoria
23. mayhem
24. legit
25. captivated
26. confounded
27. proximity
28. predicament
29. potential
30. bolstered
31. tactical
32. assassin

Chapter 6 – Choices, Decisions and Consequences

1. Define at least five characteristics of a person who is experiencing a life in jail.
2. What does the author mean when he says, "elementary understanding of religion?"
3. What is a juvenile delinquent?
4. Does death impact a change in a person's behavior?
5. Have you ever experienced a death of a loved one? Did you have a behavior change?
6. In this chapter, how does the main character describe his behavior after the death of his grandmother?
7. What is a domestic? Is there a difference between a domestic and a school custodian?
8. List some differences and some similarities betweem a domestic and a school custodian.
9. Have you ever done or thought of doing something that was against the rules? What were the consequences? Do you have any regrets?
10. What is the difference between a reformatory and a correctional facility?
11. What does the term Urban Jungle mean? Describe an Urban Jungle? Compare it to your urban neighborhood of today.
12. How could your neighborhood cause you to gravitate toward dangerous behavior?
13. Does having possession of a pistol really make your life more manageable? Why or why not?
14. What does a motorcycle sound like? Describe how a person's voice can sound like a motorcycle?
15. LeVelle Moton's mother told him it was important to have book sense, street sense and common sense. Do you think this is good advice? Why or why not?

16. What is peer pressure? Have you ever experienced being pressured by friends to do something you knew was wrong? How did you handle that pressure?
17. Can peer pressure be positive? Give an example.
18. What is the difference between a follower and a leader? What kind of person are you?

Vocabulary Words

1. intimidating
2. malicious
3. incarcerated
4. furled
5. irritated
6. rehabilitated
7. piraling
8. rebellion
9. platform
10. suppressed
11. hindsight
12. domestic
13. penitentiary
14. abuzz
15. reformatory
16. gravitated
17. petrified
18. steely
19. veneer
20. consciously
21. peer pressure
22. succumbed

Chapter 7 – Lunch Ticket (A Love Story)

1. What type of a people do the seniors remind you of? Give an example that brings you to that conclusion.
2. Why do you think Annisha broke up with LeVelle? Was it because he had to use a lunch ticket?
3. Does a coat of steel really exist? What did LeVelle Moton mean when he said he would "put on a coat of steel to shield him from heartbreak?"
4. How does LeVelle Moton use his negative experiences to still remain positive?
5. How does LeVelle Moton use his negative experiences to motivate himself?

Vocabulary Words

1. self-conscious	5. superficial	9. meddling
2. inseparable	6. degraded	10. selfless
3. ambitious	7. grudge	11. severity
4. expressive	8. vulnerability	12. motivation

Chapter 8 – First Time

1. What does LeVelle Moton mean when he says, "peer pressure can change your channel like a remote control?"
2. Identify a time when peer pressure caused you to change an idea you had, or the way you behaved. Were there positive or negative consequences to your actions?
3. Why do you think LeVelle Moton refers to having sex at a young age as a "booty trap?"
4. Besides an unwanted pregnancy, what are some other reasons LeVelle Moton avoids engaging in sexual activity as a teenager?

Vocabulary Words

1. preposterous	5. fumbled	9. confounded
2. machismo	6. suave	10. formable
3. farcical	7. restraint	11. colossal
4. regaling	8. cascaded	12. chivalry

Chapter 9 – Playground Legend

1. Do you think your talents should supersede your academics? Why or why not?
2. What choices did Gary Mattison make that prevented him from following his goals?
3. "God gives you talent, but it's your responsibility to maintain that talent." What does this statement mean? Do you agree or disagree?
4. Gary Mattison was talented and could have had a career in the NBA. What advice could you give to someone you know who is talented and making poor decisions?
5. "Nothing worth having comes easy" is a quote often associated with hard work. What does this quote mean for someone who is striving to be a good athlete, musical artist, or successful student in school?

Vocabulary Words

1. anoint
2. unanimously
3. girth
4. decanter
5. illustrious
6. emulate
7. deferring
8. athleticism
9. anchored
10. manipulate
11. confident
12. leveraging
13. epitomized
14. indelible
15. virtuosity
16. daunting

Chapter 10 – Somebody Prayed For Me

1. Why was coach Frank Williams so hard on his players?
2. What was he trying to teach them?
3. What does the word discipline mean to you?
4. Does being disciplined always need to be negative? Why or why not?
5. What did LeVelle Moton mean when he said coach Williams "stamped his large foot on my neck?"
6. How did LeVelle gain respect from the Cary High School crowd?
7. Can being a part of a team, diminish your individuality? Why or why not?
8. What kind of role model was coach Frank Williams? What examples from the text would bring you to that conclusion?
9. Why do you think coach Frank Williams told his life story to LeVelle Moton? Was he trying to make him feel bad?

Vocabulary Words

1. enticing
2. intrigued
3. self-reliant
4. cocksure
5. micromanaged
6. precise
7. stickler
8. ironclad
9. decorum
10. chiseled
11. prototype
12. humiliated
13. unappeasable
14. ferocity
15. tyranny
16. sulked
17. unorthodox
18. despised
19. solidified
20. visceral
21. composure
22. defer

Chapter 11 – Going To Meet Jay-Z (As Told by 9th Wonder)

1. How difficult is it to complete a task "on the spot?" What skills/strategies do you need?
2. Describe your emotions after sharing your "gift" with a famous person.
3. What does "dreaming in Technicolor" mean?
4. What does a good work ethic have to do with success?
5. Why is preparation important when trying to reach your goals?
6. Why is it important to adequately prepare for your future?
7. How can you use your education to prepare for your future?
8. Can being popular show off your skills?
9. Why is it better to show off your skills then to try and be popular?
10. "Let my music speak for me." What does 9th Wonder mean by this statement? What do you let speak for you?
11. What does "chance favors the well prepared" mean?

Vocabulary Words

1. mantra
2. methodical
3. self-sufficiency
4. contemplation
5. buoyant
6. magnitude
7. prestigious
8. stockpile
9. fraternize
10. self-deprecating
11. phenomenon